Simple 1-2-3

Appetizers

Publications International, Ltd.

Favorite Brand Name Recipes at www.fbnr.com

Microwave Cooking: Microwave ovens vary in wattage. Use the cooking times as guidelines and check for doneness before adding more time.

Preparation/Cooking Times: Preparation times are based on the approximate amount of time required to assemble the recipe before cooking, baking, chilling or serving. These times include preparation steps such as measuring, chopping and mixing. The fact that some preparations and cooking can be done simultaneously is taken into account. Preparation of optional ingredients and serving suggestions is not included.

Contents

Company's Coming

Grilled Lobster, Shrimp and Calamari Seviche

¾ cup fresh orange juice
⅓ cup fresh lime juice
2 tablespoons tequila
2 jalapeño peppers,*
    seeded and minced
2 tablespoons chopped
    fresh cilantro, chives
    or green onion tops
1 teaspoon honey
1 teaspoon ground cumin
1 teaspoon olive oil
10 squid, cleaned and cut
    into rings and tentacles
½ pound raw medium
    shrimp, peeled and
    deveined
2 raw lobster tails
    (8 ounces each), meat
    removed and shells
    discarded

1. To make marinade, combine orange juice, lime juice, tequila, jalapeños, cilantro and honey in medium glass bowl. Measure ¼ cup marinade into small glass bowl; stir in cumin and oil. Set aside. Refrigerate remaining marinade.

2. Prepare grill for direct grilling. Bring 1 quart water to a boil in 2-quart saucepan over high heat. Add squid; cook 30 seconds or until opaque. Drain. Rinse under cold water; drain. Add squid to refrigerated marinade.

3. Thread shrimp onto metal skewers. Brush shrimp and lobster with reserved ¼ cup marinade. Place shrimp on grid. Grill shrimp on uncovered grill, over medium-hot coals, 2 to 3 minutes per side or until shrimp turn pink and opaque. Remove shrimp from skewers; add to squid. Place lobster on grid. Grill 5 minutes per side or until meat turns opaque and is cooked through. Slice lobster meat into ¼-inch-thick slices; add to squid and shrimp mixture. Refrigerate at least 2 hours or overnight. *Makes 6 servings*

Jalapeño peppers can sting and irritate the skin. Wear rubber gloves when handling peppers and do not touch eyes. Wash hands after handling.

1 cup shredded cabbage or coleslaw mix

½ cup finely chopped cooked ham

¼ cup finely chopped water chestnuts

¼ cup thinly sliced green onions

3 tablespoons plum sauce, divided

1 teaspoon dark sesame oil

3 (6-inch) flour tortillas

Spring Rolls

1. Combine cabbage, ham, water chestnuts, onions, 2 tablespoons plum sauce and sesame oil in medium bowl. Mix well. Spread remaining 1 tablespoon plum sauce evenly over tortillas.

2. Spread about ½ cup cabbage mixture onto each tortilla to within ¼ inch of edge; roll up. Wrap each tortilla roll tightly in plastic wrap. Refrigerate at least 1 hour or up to 24 hours before serving.

3. Cut each tortilla roll diagonally into 4 pieces.   *Makes 12 appetizers*

Company's Coming

Stout Beef Bundles

1. Brown ground beef in medium skillet over medium-high heat; drain fat. Add onions and garlic; cook and stir until tender.

2. Stir in water chestnuts, bell pepper, stout, hoisin and soy sauce. Cook, stirring occasionally, until bell pepper is crisp-tender and most of liquid has evaporated. Remove from heat. Stir in cilantro.

3. Spoon ground beef mixture onto lettuce leaves; sprinkle with additional hoisin sauce, if desired. Wrap lettuce leaf around ground beef mixture to make appetizer bundle.

Makes 8 servings

Tip: Slice additional green onions into long strips and use to tie bundles.

1 pound ground beef
½ cup sliced green onions
1 medium clove garlic, minced
⅔ cup chopped water chestnuts
½ cup chopped red bell pepper
¼ cup stout beer
2 tablespoons hoisin sauce
1 tablespoon soy sauce
2 tablespoons chopped fresh cilantro
1 or 2 heads leaf lettuce, separated into leaves, outer leaves discarded

Company's Coming

Tuna in Crispy Wonton Cups

18 wonton skins, each
    3¼ inches square
    Butter or olive oil
    cooking spray
1 (3-ounce) pouch of
    STARKIST® Premium
    Albacore or Chunk
    Light Tuna
⅓ cup cold cooked orzo
    (rice-shaped pasta) or
    cooked rice
¼ cup southwestern ranch-
    style vegetable dip
    with jalapeños or other
    sour cream dip
¼ cup drained pimiento-
    stuffed green olives,
    chopped
3 tablespoons sweet pickle
    relish, drained

Cut wontons into circles with 3-inch round cookie cutter. Spray miniature muffin pans with cooking spray. Place one circle in each muffin cup; press to sides to mold wonton to cup. Spray each wonton with cooking spray. Bake in 350°F oven 6 to 8 minutes or until golden brown; set aside.

In small bowl, gently mix tuna, orzo, dip, olives and relish. Refrigerate filling until ready to serve.

Remove won ton cups from muffin pan. Use rounded teaspoon to fill each cup; garnish with paprika and parsley.   *Makes 18 servings*

Tip: Cups may be made a day ahead; store in airtight container. Reheat in 350°F oven 1 to 2 minutes to recrisp.

Prep Time: *20 minutes*

Company's Coming

Portobello Mushrooms Sesame

1. Prepare grill for direct grilling.

2. Remove and discard stems from mushrooms; set caps aside. Combine remaining ingredients in small bowl.

3. Brush both sides of mushroom caps with soy sauce mixture. Grill mushrooms, top side up, on covered grill over medium coals 3 to 4 minutes. Brush tops with soy sauce mixture; turn over. Grill 2 minutes more or until mushrooms are lightly browned. Turn again; grill, basting frequently, 4 to 5 minutes or until tender when pressed with back of spatula. Remove mushrooms; cut diagonally into ½-inch-thick slices.   *Makes 4 servings*

4 large portobello
   mushrooms
2 tablespoons sweet rice
   wine
2 tablespoons soy sauce
2 cloves garlic, minced
1 teaspoon dark sesame oil

•9•

Company's Coming

Turkey-Broccoli Roll-Ups

2 pounds broccoli spears
⅓ cup sour cream
¼ cup mayonnaise
2 tablespoons thawed frozen orange juice concentrate
1 tablespoon Dijon mustard
1 teaspoon dried basil leaves
1 pound smoked turkey, very thinly sliced

Microwave Directions

1. Arrange broccoli spears in single layer in large, shallow microwavable dish. Add 1 tablespoon water. Cover dish tightly with plastic wrap; vent. Microwave at HIGH 6 to 7 minutes or just until broccoli is crisp-tender, rearranging spears after 4 minutes. Carefully remove plastic wrap; drain broccoli. Immediately place broccoli in cold water to stop cooking; drain well. Pat dry with paper towels.

2. Combine sour cream, mayonnaise, juice concentrate, mustard and basil in small bowl.

3. Cut turkey slices into 2-inch-wide strips. Spread sour cream mixture evenly onto strips. Place 1 broccoli spear at short end of each strip. Starting at short end, roll up tightly, allowing broccoli spear to protrude from one end. Place on serving platter; cover with plastic wrap. Refrigerate until ready to serve. Garnish just before serving, if desired. *Makes 20 servings*

Note: To blanch broccoli on stove top, bring small amount of water to a boil in saucepan. Add broccoli spears; cover. Simmer 2 to 3 minutes or until broccoli is crisp-tender. Immediately place broccoli in cold water to stop cooking; drain well. Continue as directed.

Company's Coming

Chicken and Rice Puffs

1. Bake pastry shells according to package directions. Keep warm.

2. Prepare rice according to package directions.

3. Add remaining ingredients to rice; mix well. Cook over medium heat 4 to 5 minutes or until hot and bubbly. Fill pastry shells with rice mixture. Serve immediately.

Makes 6 servings

Tip: This is a great way to use leftover chicken.

1 box frozen puff pastry shells, thawed

1 package (about 6 ounces) long grain and wild rice

2 cups cubed cooked chicken

½ (10¾-ounce) can condensed cream of chicken soup, undiluted

⅓ cup chopped slivered almonds, toasted

⅓ cup *each* diced celery and diced red bell pepper

⅓ cup chopped fresh parsley

¼ cup diced onion

¼ cup white wine or chicken broth

Company's Coming

Southern Crab Cakes with Rémoulade Dipping Sauce

10 ounces fresh lump
   crabmeat
1½ cups fresh white or
   sourdough bread
   crumbs, divided
¼ cup chopped green
   onions
½ cup mayonnaise, divided
1 egg white, lightly beaten
2 tablespoons coarse grain
   or spicy brown
   mustard, divided
¾ teaspoon hot pepper
   sauce, divided
2 teaspoons olive oil,
   divided
   Lemon wedges

1. Preheat oven to 200°F. Combine crabmeat, ¾ cup bread crumbs and green onions in medium bowl. Add ¼ cup mayonnaise, egg white, 1 tablespoon mustard and ½ teaspoon pepper sauce; mix well. Using ¼ cup mixture per cake, shape into 8 (½-inch-thick) cakes. Roll crab cakes lightly in remaining ¾ cup bread crumbs.

2. Heat large nonstick skillet over medium heat until hot; add 1 teaspoon oil. Add 4 crab cakes; cook 4 to 5 minutes per side or until golden brown. Transfer to ovenproof serving platter; keep warm in oven. Repeat with remaining 1 teaspoon oil and crab cakes.

3. To prepare dipping sauce, combine remaining ¼ cup mayonnaise, 1 tablespoon mustard and ¼ teaspoon hot pepper sauce in small bowl; mix well. Serve crab cakes warm with lemon wedges and dipping sauce.

Makes 8 servings

Artichoke Frittata

1. Chop artichoke hearts; set aside.

2. Heat 2 teaspoons oil in 10-inch skillet over medium heat. Add green onions; cook and stir until tender. Remove from skillet. Beat eggs in medium bowl until light. Stir in artichokes, green onions, cheeses, parsley, salt and pepper to taste.

3. Heat remaining 1 teaspoon oil in same skillet over medium heat. Pour egg mixture into skillet. Cook 4 to 5 minutes or until bottom is lightly browned. Place large plate over skillet; invert frittata onto plate. Return frittata, uncooked side down, to skillet. Cook about 4 minutes more or until center is just set. Cut into small wedges. *Makes 12 to 16 servings*

1 can (14 ounces) artichoke hearts, drained
3 teaspoons olive oil, divided
½ cup minced green onions
5 eggs
½ cup (2 ounces) shredded Swiss cheese
2 tablespoons grated Parmesan cheese
1 tablespoon minced fresh parsley
1 teaspoon salt
Black pepper

Company's Coming

Egg Champignons

6 eggs, hard cooked,
   peeled and chopped
¼ cup dry bread crumbs
¼ cup (1 ounce) crumbled
   blue cheese
2 tablespoons thinly sliced
   green onions with tops
2 tablespoons dry white
   wine
2 tablespoons butter, melted
1 tablespoon chopped
   fresh parsley *or*
   1½ teaspoons dried
   parsley flakes
½ teaspoon garlic salt
24 large mushroom caps
   (about 1½ inches in
   diameter)
   Paprika (optional)
   Green onions and tomato
   slices, for garnish

1. Preheat oven to 450°F. Lightly grease baking sheet. Combine eggs, bread crumbs, blue cheese, 2 tablespoons green onions, wine, butter, parsley and garlic salt in medium bowl.

2. Place mushroom caps on prepared baking sheet. Fill each cap with 1 rounded tablespoonful egg mixture.

3. Bake 8 to 10 minutes. Sprinkle with paprika and garnish, if desired.

Makes 8 servings

Baked Spinach Balls

1. Combine bread stuffing mix, onion, cheese, garlic, thyme and pepper in medium bowl; mix well. Combine spinach, broth and egg whites in separate medium bowl; mix well. Stir into bread cube mixture. Cover; refrigerate 1 hour or until mixture is firm.

2. Preheat oven to 350°F. Shape mixture into 24 balls; place on ungreased baking sheet. Bake 15 minutes or until spinach balls are browned.

3. Serve with mustard for dipping, if desired. Garnish, if desired.

Makes 12 servings

2 cups sage and onion or herb-seasoned bread stuffing mix
1 small onion, chopped
2 tablespoons grated Parmesan cheese
1 clove garlic, minced
¼ teaspoon dried thyme leaves
¼ teaspoon black pepper
1 package (10 ounces) frozen chopped spinach, thawed and well drained
¼ cup fat-free reduced-sodium chicken broth
2 egg whites, beaten
Dijon or honey mustard (optional)

Company's Coming

Vegetable & Couscous Filled Tomatoes

½ cup reduced-sodium
  chicken broth
2 teaspoons olive oil
⅓ cup uncooked couscous
18 large plum tomatoes
  Nonstick cooking spray
1 cup diced zucchini
⅓ cup sliced green onions
2 cloves garlic, minced
2 tablespoons finely
  chopped fresh Italian
  parsley
1½ teaspoons Dijon mustard
½ teaspoon dried Italian
  seasoning

1. Place chicken broth and oil in small saucepan; bring to a boil over high heat. Stir in couscous; cover. Remove saucepan from heat; let stand 5 minutes. Meanwhile, cut thin slice from top of each tomato. Remove pulp, leaving ⅛-inch-thick shell; reserve pulp. Place tomatoes, cut side down, on paper towels to drain. Meanwhile, drain excess liquid from reserved pulp. Chop pulp to measure ⅔ cup.

2. Spray large nonstick skillet with cooking spray; heat over medium heat until hot. Add zucchini, onions and garlic. Cook and stir 5 minutes or until vegetables are tender.

3. Combine couscous, reserved tomato pulp, vegetables, parsley, mustard and Italian seasoning in large bowl. Fill tomato shells with couscous mixture. Garnish as desired. *Makes 18 servings*

Company's Coming

Tuscan Tuna Stuffed Pasta Salad

Cook pasta shells according to package directions, using shortest cooking time. Drain; rinse under cold running water. Set aside.

Combine salad dressing, basil, salt and pepper in medium bowl; whisk until well blended. Stir in beans, tuna, pimiento and ⅔ cup French Fried Onions.

Spoon 3 tablespoons bean mixture into each pasta shell. Sprinkle with remaining ⅔ cup onions.   *Makes 8 appetizer servings*

Prep Time: *20 minutes*
Cook Time: *10 minutes*

16 uncooked jumbo pasta shells
½ cup balsamic vinaigrette salad dressing
¼ cup chopped fresh basil or parsley
½ teaspoon salt
⅛ teaspoon ground black pepper
1 can (15 ounces) white kidney beans, rinsed and drained
1 can (6 ounces) white tuna packed in water, drained and flaked
1 jar (4 ounces) chopped pimiento, rinsed and drained
1⅓ cups *French's*® French Fried Onions, divided

Venetian Canapés

12 slices firm white bread
5 tablespoons butter or margarine, divided
2 tablespoons all-purpose flour
½ cup milk
3 ounces fresh mushrooms (about 9 medium), finely chopped
6 tablespoons shredded Parmesan cheese, divided
2 teaspoons anchovy paste
¼ teaspoon salt
⅛ teaspoon black pepper
Green and ripe black olive slices, red and green bell pepper strips and rolled anchovy fillets, for garnish

1. Preheat oven to 350°F. Cut 2 rounds out of each bread slice with 2-inch round cutter. Melt 3 tablespoons butter in small saucepan. Brush both sides of bread rounds lightly with butter. Bake bread rounds on ungreased baking sheet 5 to 6 minutes per side or until golden. Remove to wire rack. Cool completely. *Increase oven temperature to 425°F.*

2. Melt remaining 2 tablespoons butter in same small saucepan. Stir in flour; cook and stir over medium heat until bubbly. Whisk in milk; cook and stir 1 minute or until sauce thickens and bubbles. (Sauce will be very thick.) Place mushrooms in large bowl; stir in sauce, 3 tablespoons cheese, anchovy paste, salt and black pepper until well blended.

3. Spread 1 heaping teaspoonful mushroom mixture onto each toast round; place on ungreased baking sheets. Sprinkle remaining 3 tablespoons cheese over bread rounds. Bake 5 to 7 minutes or until tops are light brown. Serve warm. Garnish, if desired.   *Makes 8 to 10 servings (about 2 dozen)*

Anchovy Paste

Smoked Salmon Appetizers

1. Combine cream cheese, dill and red pepper in small bowl; stir to blend. Spread evenly over each slice of salmon. Roll up salmon slices jelly-roll style. Place on plate; cover with plastic wrap. Chill at least 1 hour or up to 4 hours before serving.

2. Using sharp knife, cut salmon rolls crosswise into ³⁄₄-inch pieces. Place pieces, cut side down, on melba rounds.

3. Garnish each salmon roll with dill sprig, if desired. Serve cold or at room temperature. *Makes about 2 dozen appetizers*

¼ **cup reduced-fat or fat-free cream cheese, softened**
1 **tablespoon chopped fresh dill** *or* **1 teaspoon dried dill weed**
⅛ **teaspoon ground red pepper**
4 **ounces thinly sliced smoked salmon or lox**
24 **melba toast rounds or other low-fat crackers**
Fresh dill sprigs, for garnish (optional)

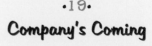

Roasted Eggplant Rolls

2 medium eggplants
(¾ pound each)
2 tablespoons lemon juice
1 teaspoon olive oil
4 tablespoons (2 ounces)
fat-free cream cheese
2 tablespoons fat-free sour
cream
1 green onion, minced
4 sun-dried tomatoes
(packed in oil), rinsed,
drained and minced
1 clove garlic, minced
¼ teaspoon dried oregano
leaves
⅛ teaspoon black pepper
16 medium spinach leaves,
washed, stemmed and
dried
1 cup bottled spaghetti
sauce

1. Preheat oven to 450°F. Spray 2 nonstick baking sheets with nonstick cooking spray; set aside. Trim ends from eggplants. Cut eggplants lengthwise into ¼-inch-thick slices. Discard outside slices that are mostly skin. (You will have about 16 slices.) Arrange slices in single layer on prepared baking sheets.

2. Combine lemon juice and olive oil in small bowl; brush lightly over both sides of eggplant slices. Bake 22 to 24 minutes or until slightly golden brown, turning once. Transfer eggplant slices to plate; cool. Meanwhile, stir together cream cheese, sour cream, green onion, sun-dried tomatoes, garlic, oregano and pepper in small bowl until blended.

3. Spread about 1 teaspoon cream cheese mixture evenly over each eggplant slice. Arrange spinach leaf on top, leaving ½-inch border. Roll up, beginning at small end. Lay rolls, seam side down, on serving platter. (If making ahead, cover and refrigerate up to 2 days. Bring to room temperature before serving.) Serve with warm spaghetti sauce. *Makes 8 servings (16 rolls)*

Spanish-Style Garlic Shrimp

In 12-inch nonstick skillet, melt 1 tablespoon I Can't Believe It's Not Butter!® Spread over high heat and cook shrimp with salt 2 minutes or until shrimp are almost pink, turning once. Remove shrimp and set aside.

In same skillet, melt remaining 3 tablespoons I Can't Believe It's Not Butter!® Spread over medium-low heat and cook garlic and jalapeño pepper, stirring occasionally, 1 minute. Return shrimp to skillet. Stir in cilantro and lime juice and heat 30 seconds or until shrimp turn pink.

Serve, if desired, with crusty Italian bread.   *Makes 6 servings*

- **4 tablespoons I CAN'T BELIEVE IT'S NOT BUTTER!® Spread, divided**
- **1 pound uncooked medium shrimp, peeled and deveined**
- **½ teaspoon salt**
- **2 cloves garlic, finely chopped**
- **½ to 1 jalapeño pepper, seeded and finely chopped**
- **¼ cup chopped fresh cilantro or parsley**
- **1 tablespoon fresh lime juice**

Roasted Red Pepper and Artichoke Torte

2½ cups chopped bagels (about 3 bagels)

2 tablespoons olive oil

2 packages (8 ounces each) cream cheese, softened

1 container (15 ounces) ricotta cheese

1 can (10¾ ounces) condensed cream of celery soup, undiluted

2 eggs *or* ½ cup cholesterol-free egg substitute

2 tablespoons chopped green onion

1 tablespoon dried Italian seasoning

1 clove garlic, minced

1 can (8½ ounces) artichoke hearts, drained and chopped

1 jar (15 ounces) roasted red bell peppers, drained, chopped and divided

1 cup chopped fresh basil, divided

1. Preheat oven to 375°F. Combine bagels and oil in medium bowl; mix well. Spray 9×2½-inch springform baking pan with nonstick cooking spray. Press bagel mixture into bottom of prepared pan. Bake 15 minutes; cool.

2. Beat cheeses, soup, eggs, green onion, Italian seasoning and garlic with electric mixer at medium speed until well blended. Spread half of cheese mixture over bagel crust. Top with artichokes and half *each* of peppers and basil. Spread remaining cheese mixture over basil; top with remaining peppers.

3. Bake 1 hour or until center is set; cool. Refrigerate 6 to 8 hours or overnight. Run knife around edge of torte; remove side of pan. Top with remaining ½ cup basil. Slice thinly; serve with crackers. *Makes 20 servings*

Cranberry-Walnut Pear Wedges

1. Place pears in large resealable plastic food storage bag. Pour liqueur and orange juice over pears; seal bag. Turn bag several times to coat pears evenly. Refrigerate at least 1 hour, turning bag occasionally.

2. Drain pears; discard marinade.

3. Place pears on serving platter. Spoon cranberry relish evenly into cavities of pears; sprinkle with walnuts and cheese. Garnish, if desired.

Makes 12 servings

*Omit liqueur, if desired. Increase orange juice to ¼ cup. Add 2 tablespoons honey and 2 tablespoons balsamic vinegar to marinade.

3 firm ripe pears, cut into quarters and cored
¼ cup triple sec*
2 tablespoons orange juice
½ cup prepared cranberry fruit relish
¼ cup finely chopped walnuts
¼ cup (1 ounce) crumbled blue cheese

Jicama & Shrimp Cocktail with Roasted Red Pepper Sauce

2 large red bell peppers
6 ounces (about
    24 medium to large)
    shrimp, peeled and
    deveined
1 medium clove garlic
1½ cups fresh cilantro sprigs
2 tablespoons lime juice
2 tablespoons orange juice
½ teaspoon hot pepper
    sauce
1 small jicama (about
    ¾ pound), peeled and
    cut into strips
1 plum tomato, halved,
    seeded and thinly
    sliced
    Lettuce leaves (optional)

1. Preheat broiler. Place bell peppers on broiler pan. Broil 4 to 6 inches from heat about 6 minutes, turning every 2 to 3 minutes or until all sides are charred. Transfer peppers to paper bag; close bag tightly. Let stand 10 minutes or until peppers are cool enough to handle and skins are loosened. Peel peppers. Cut peppers in half. Remove cores, seeds and membranes; discard.

2. Add shrimp to large saucepan of boiling water. Reduce heat to medium-low; simmer, uncovered, 2 to 3 minutes or until shrimp turn pink. Drain shrimp; rinse under cold running water. Cover; refrigerate until ready to use.

3. Place peppers and garlic in food processor. Cover; process until coarsely chopped. Add cilantro, lime juice, orange juice and pepper sauce; process until cilantro is finely chopped but mixture is not puréed. Combine jicama, shrimp and tomato in large bowl. Add bell pepper mixture; toss to coat. Serve over lettuce and garnish with red bell pepper strips, if desired.   *Makes 8 servings*

Company's Coming

Devilish Eggs

1. Remove yolk from egg whites using teaspoon. Press yolks through sieve with back of spoon or mash with fork in medium bowl. Stir in mayonnaise, mustard, salt and pepper; mix well.

2. Spoon or pipe yolk mixture into egg whites. Arrange on serving platter. Garnish as desired.

3. Cover; chill in refrigerator until ready to serve.

Makes 12 servings

Zesty Variations: Stir in one of the following: 2 tablespoons minced red onion plus 1 tablespoon horseradish, 2 tablespoons pickle relish plus 1 tablespoon minced fresh dill, 2 tablespoons each minced onion and celery plus 1 tablespoon minced fresh dill, ¼ cup (1 ounce) shredded Cheddar cheese plus ½ teaspoon *French's®* Worcestershire Sauce.

Prep Time: *40 minutes*
Chill Time: *30 minutes*

12 hard-cooked eggs, cut in half
6 tablespoons low-fat mayonnaise
2 tablespoons *French's®* Classic Yellow® Mustard
¼ teaspoon salt
⅛ teaspoon ground red pepper

Company's Coming

Roasted Garlic and Spinach Spirals

1 whole head fresh garlic
3 cups fresh spinach leaves
1 can (15 ounces) white
    beans, rinsed and
    drained
1 teaspoon dried oregano
    leaves
¼ teaspoon black pepper
⅛ teaspoon ground red
    pepper
7 (7-inch) flour tortillas

1. Preheat oven to 400°F. Trim tops off garlic cloves; discard. Moisten head of garlic with water; wrap in foil. Bake 45 minutes or until garlic is soft; cool.

2. Meanwhile, rinse spinach leaves; pat dry with paper towels. Remove stems; discard. Finely shred leaves. Place in medium bowl.

3. Remove garlic from skin. Place garlic in food processor. Add beans, oregano, black pepper and red pepper. Cover; process until smooth. Add to spinach; mix well. Spread mixture evenly onto tortillas; roll up jelly-roll style.* Trim ½ inch off ends of rolls; discard. Cut rolls into 1-inch pieces. Transfer to serving plates; garnish, if desired. *Makes 10 servings*

For best results, at this point, cover tortilla rolls and refrigerate 1 to 2 hours before slicing.

Company's Coming

Brandy-Soaked Scallops

1. Wrap one piece bacon around each scallop; secure with toothpick, if necessary. Place wrapped scallops in 13×9-inch baking dish.

2. Combine brandy, oil, parsley, garlic, pepper, salt and onion powder in small bowl; mix well. Pour mixture over scallops; cover and marinate in refrigerator at least 4 hours.

3. Remove scallops from marinade; discard marinade. Arrange scallops on rack of broiler pan. Broil 4 inches from heat 7 to 10 minutes or until bacon is brown. Turn over; broil 5 minutes more or until scallops are opaque. Remove toothpicks before serving. Arrange over salad greens and garnish, if desired.

Makes 8 servings

1 pound bacon, cut in half crosswise
2 pounds small sea scallops
½ cup brandy
⅓ cup olive oil
2 tablespoons chopped fresh parsley
1 clove garlic, minced
1 teaspoon black pepper
½ teaspoon salt
½ teaspoon onion powder
Salad greens (optional)

Company's Coming

1 zucchini, cut lengthwise
    into ¼-inch-thick slices
Nonstick cooking spray
3 shiitake mushrooms
4 large sweet onions
1 plum tomato, seeded and
    chopped
2 tablespoons fresh bread
    crumbs
1 tablespoon fresh basil *or*
    1 teaspoon dried basil
    leaves
1 teaspoon olive oil
¼ teaspoon salt
⅛ teaspoon black pepper
4 teaspoons balsamic
    vinegar

Savory Herb-Stuffed Onions

1. Prepare grill for direct grilling. Spray both sides of zucchini slices with cooking spray. Grill on uncovered grill over medium coals 4 minutes or until tender, turning once. Remove; cool. Cut into bite-size pieces; set aside. Thread mushrooms onto metal skewers. Grill on covered grill over medium coals 20 to 30 minutes or until tender. Remove; coarsely chop. Set aside.

2. Remove stem and root ends of onions, leaving peels intact. Spray onions with cooking spray; grill, root end up, on covered grill over medium coals 5 minutes or until lightly charred. Remove; cool slightly. Peel and scoop about 1 inch of pulp from stem ends; chop pulp for filling.

3. Combine zucchini, mushrooms, onion, tomato, bread crumbs, basil, oil, salt and pepper in large bowl; mix until well blended. Spoon equal amounts of stuffing mixture into centers of onions. Place each onion on sheet of foil; sprinkle each with 1 tablespoon water. Wrap onions; seal foil. Grill onion packets on covered grill over medium coals 45 to 60 minutes or until tender. Spoon 1 teaspoon vinegar over each onion before serving. *Makes 4 servings*

Company's Coming

Sesame Pork Appetizers

Place pork in large plastic bag. Combine ½ cup of the sherry and 1 tablespoon of the soy sauce; pour over pork, turning to coat. Tie bag. Marinate in refrigerator 1 to 2 hours, turning several times.

Remove pork from marinade. Discard marinade. Spread honey on plate. Spread sesame seeds in shallow dish. Roll pork in honey, then in sesame seeds. Arrange pork on roasting rack set in roasting pan. Bake at 350°F 25 to 30 minutes or until meat thermometer registers 155°F. Let stand 5 minutes. Slice thinly on the diagonal. Set aside.

Combine remaining ⅓ cup soy sauce, remaining 1 tablespoon sherry, the sesame oil, garlic, ginger and onion in small bowl. Place bowl in center of serving platter. Surround bowl with spinach leaves. Arrange pork slices on top.

Makes 10 to 12 appetizer servings

Favorite recipe from **National Pork Board**

1½ **pounds pork tenderloin**
½ **cup plus 1 tablespoon dry sherry, divided**
⅓ **cup plus 1 tablespoon soy sauce, divided**
½ **cup honey**
½ **cup sesame seeds**
1 **tablespoon sesame oil**
1 **clove garlic, crushed**
½ **teaspoon grated fresh ginger**
1 **green onion, finely chopped**
Spinach leaves

Company's Coming

Filled & Skewered

Spinach-Artichoke Party Cups

Nonstick cooking spray
36 (3-inch) wonton wrappers
1 can (8½ ounces)
    artichoke hearts,
    drained and chopped
½ (10-ounce) package
    frozen chopped
    spinach, thawed and
    squeezed dry
1 cup shredded Monterey
    Jack cheese
½ cup grated Parmesan
    cheese
½ cup mayonnaise
1 clove garlic, minced

1. Preheat oven to 300°F. Spray miniature muffin pan lightly with cooking spray. Press 1 wonton wrapper into each cup; spray lightly with cooking spray. Bake about 9 minutes or until light golden brown. Remove shells from muffin pan; set aside to cool. Repeat with remaining wonton wrappers.*

2. Meanwhile, combine artichoke hearts, spinach, cheeses, mayonnaise and garlic in medium bowl; mix well.

3. Fill each wonton cup with about 1½ teaspoons spinach-artichoke mixture. Place filled cups on baking sheet. Bake about 7 minutes or until heated through. Serve immediately.   *Makes 36 appetizers*

Wonton cups may be prepared up to one week in advance. Cool completely and store in an airtight container.

Tip: If you have leftover spinach-artichoke mixture after filling the wonton cups, place the mixture in a shallow ovenproof dish and bake it at 350°F until hot and bubbly. Serve it with bread or crackers.

Honeyed Pork and Mango Kabobs

½ cup honey

¼ cup frozen apple juice concentrate, thawed

3 tablespoons *Frank's® RedHot®* Original Cayenne Pepper Sauce

¼ teaspoon ground allspice

1 teaspoon grated lemon peel

1 pound pork tenderloin, cut into 1-inch cubes

1 large (12 ounces) ripe mango, peeled, pitted and cut into ¾-inch cubes, divided

½ cup frozen large baby onions, partially thawed

1. Combine honey, juice concentrate, **Frank's RedHot** Sauce and allspice in small saucepan. Bring to a boil over medium heat. Reduce heat to low; cook, stirring, 5 minutes. Stir in lemon peel. Remove from heat. Pour ¼ cup marinade into small bowl; reserve. Place pork in large resealable plastic food storage bag. Pour remaining marinade over pork. Seal bag; refrigerate 1 hour. Prepare grill.

2. To prepare dipping sauce, place ¼ cup mango cubes in blender or food processor. Add reserved ¼ cup marinade. Cover; process until puréed. Transfer to serving bowl; set aside.

3. Alternately thread pork, remaining mango cubes and onions onto metal skewers. Place skewers on oiled grid. Grill,* over medium-low coals, 12 to 15 minutes or until pork is no longer pink. Serve kabobs with dipping sauce.

Makes 6 servings (¾ cup sauce)

*Or, broil 6 inches from heat 10 to 12 minutes or until pork is no longer pink.

Note: Substitute 1½ cups fresh or frozen peach cubes (2 to 3 peaches) for fresh mango, if desired.

Prep Time: *30 minutes*
Marinate Time: *1 hour*
Cook Time: *about 20 minutes*

Filled & Skewered

Easy Sausage Empanadas

Let pie crusts stand at room temperature for 20 minutes or according to package directions.

Crumble sausage into medium skillet. Add onion, garlic powder, cumin and oregano; cook over medium-high heat until sausage is no longer pink. Drain drippings. Stir in olives and raisins. Beat the egg yolk slightly; stir into sausage mixture, mixing well.

Carefully unfold crusts. Cut into desired shapes using 3-inch cookie cutters. Place about 2 teaspoons of the sausage filling on half the cutouts. Top with remaining cutouts. (Or, use round cutter, top with sausage filling and fold dough over to create half-moon shape.) Moisten fingers with water and pinch dough to seal edges. Slightly beat the egg white; gently brush over tops of empanadas. Bake in a 425°F oven 15 to 18 minutes or until golden brown.

Makes 12 appetizer servings

Prep Time: *25 minutes*
Cook Time: *15 minutes*

Favorite recipe from **National Pork Board**

¼ **pound bulk pork sausage**
1 **(15-ounce) package refrigerated pie crusts (2 crusts)**
2 **tablespoons finely chopped onion**
⅛ **teaspoon garlic powder**
⅛ **teaspoon ground cumin**
⅛ **teaspoon dried oregano, crushed**
1 **tablespoon chopped pimiento-stuffed olives**
1 **tablespoon chopped raisins**
1 **egg, separated**

Filled & Skewered

Herb Cheese Twists

2 tablespoons butter or margarine

¼ cup grated Parmesan cheese

1 teaspoon dried parsley flakes

1 teaspoon dried basil leaves

1 can (7½ ounces) refrigerated buttermilk biscuits

1. Preheat oven to 400°F. Microwave butter in small bowl at MEDIUM (50% power) just until melted; cool slightly. Stir in cheese, parsley and basil. Set aside.

2. Pat each biscuit into 5×2-inch rectangle. Spread 1 teaspoon butter mixture onto each rectangle; cut each in half lengthwise. Twist each strip 3 or 4 times.

3. Place on lightly greased baking sheet. Bake 8 to 10 minutes or until golden brown. *Makes 5 servings*

Hint: Save even more time by using ready-to-bake breadsticks. Spread the butter mixture onto the breadsticks, then bake them according to the package directions.

Filled & Skewered

Leek Strudels

1. Coat large skillet with nonstick cooking spray; heat over medium heat. Add leeks; cook and stir about 5 minutes or until tender. Stir in caraway seeds, salt and pepper. Add chicken broth; bring to a boil over high heat. Reduce heat to low. Simmer, covered, about 5 minutes or until broth is absorbed. Let cool to room temperature.

2. Preheat oven to 400°F. Cut each sheet of phyllo lengthwise into thirds. Spray 1 piece phyllo dough with nonstick cooking spray; spoon 2 tablespoons leek mixture onto bottom of piece. Fold 1 corner over filling to make triangle. Continue folding, as you would fold a flag, to make triangular packet.

3. Repeat with remaining phyllo dough and leek mixture. Place packets on cookie sheet; lightly coat tops of packets with butter-flavored cooking spray. Bake about 20 minutes or until golden brown. Serve warm.

Makes 9 servings

Nonstick cooking spray
2 pounds leeks, cleaned and sliced (white parts only)
¼ teaspoon caraway seeds
¼ teaspoon salt
⅛ teaspoon white pepper
¼ cup fat-free reduced-sodium chicken broth
3 sheets frozen phyllo dough, thawed
Butter-flavored nonstick cooking spray

Filled & Skewered

Spicy Tuna Empanadas

1 (3-ounce) pouch of
    STARKIST® Premium
    Albacore or Chunk
    Light Tuna
1 can (4 ounces) diced
    green chilies, drained
1 can (2¼ ounces) sliced
    ripe olives, drained
½ cup shredded sharp
    Cheddar cheese
1 chopped hard-cooked egg
    Salt and pepper to taste
¼ teaspoon hot pepper
    sauce
¼ cup medium thick and
    chunky salsa
2 packages (15 ounces
    each) refrigerated pie
    crusts
    Additional salsa

In medium bowl, place tuna, chilies, olives, cheese, egg, salt, pepper and hot pepper sauce; toss lightly with fork. Add ¼ cup salsa and toss again; set aside.

Following directions on package, unfold pie crusts (roll out slightly with rolling pin if you prefer thinner crust); cut 4 circles, 4 inches each, out of each crust. Place 8 circles on foil-covered baking sheets; wet edge of each circle with water. Top each circle with ¼ cup lightly packed tuna mixture. Top with remaining circles, stretching pastry slightly to fit; press edges together and crimp with fork. Cut slits in top crust to vent.

Bake in 425°F oven 15 to 18 minutes or until golden brown. Cool slightly. Serve with additional salsa.   *Makes 8 servings*

Filled & Skewered

Mini Marinated Beef Skewers

1. Preheat broiler. Cut beef crosswise into 18 (⅛-inch-thick) slices. Place in large resealable plastic food storage bag. Combine soy sauce, sherry, oil and garlic in cup; pour over beef. Seal bag; turn to coat. Marinate in refrigerator at least 30 minutes or up to 2 hours.

2. Soak 18 (6-inch) wooden skewers in water 20 minutes. Preheat broiler. Drain beef; discard marinade. Weave beef accordion-style onto skewers. Place on rack of broiler pan. Broil 4 to 5 inches from heat 2 minutes. Turn skewers over; broil 2 minutes more or until beef is barely pink.

3. Garnish each skewer with 1 cherry tomato and place on lettuce-lined platter, if desired. Serve warm. *Makes 6 servings (3 skewers each)*

1 beef top round steak
   (about 1 pound)
2 tablespoons soy sauce
1 tablespoon dry sherry
1 teaspoon dark sesame oil
2 cloves garlic, minced
18 cherry tomatoes
   (optional)
   Lettuce (optional)

Nonstick cooking spray
20 (3-inch) wonton
   wrappers
1 tablespoon sesame seeds
2 boneless skinless chicken
   breasts (about
   8 ounces)
1 cup fresh green beans,
   cut diagonally into
   ½-inch pieces
¼ cup mayonnaise
1 tablespoon chopped
   fresh cilantro
   (optional)
2 teaspoons honey
1 teaspoon reduced-
   sodium soy sauce
⅛ teaspoon ground red
   pepper

Filled & Skewered

Sesame Chicken Salad Wonton Cups

1. Preheat oven to 350°F. Spray miniature muffin pan with cooking spray. Press 1 wonton wrapper into each muffin cup; spray with cooking spray. Bake 8 to 10 minutes or until golden brown. Cool in pan on wire rack. Place sesame seeds in shallow baking pan. Bake 5 minutes or until lightly toasted, stirring occasionally. Set aside to cool.

2. Meanwhile, bring 2 cups water to a boil in medium saucepan. Add chicken. Reduce heat to low. Cover; simmer 10 minutes or until chicken is no longer pink in center, adding green beans after 7 minutes. Drain.

3. Finely chop chicken. Place in medium bowl. Add green beans and remaining ingredients; mix lightly. Spoon lightly rounded tablespoonful chicken mixture into each wonton cup. Garnish, if desired. *Makes 10 servings*

Mini Taco Quiches

1. Preheat oven to 350°F. Grease 12 muffin pan cups. Set aside.

2. Cook beef and onions in large nonstick skillet until meat is browned; drain. Remove from heat. Stir in olives, tomato sauce, ¼ cup water, taco seasoning, *Frank's RedHot* Sauce and egg; mix well.

3. Using 4-inch cookie cutter, cut each flour tortilla into 3 rounds. Fit tortilla rounds into prepared muffin cups. Fill each tortilla cup with ¼ cup meat mixture. Top each with sour cream and cheese. Bake 25 minutes or until heated through.

Makes 12 servings

Prep Time: *20 minutes*
Cook Time: *30 minutes*

1 pound lean ground beef
¹⁄₃ cup chopped onions
¹⁄₃ cup sliced black olives
1 can (8 ounces) tomato sauce
1 package (1¼ ounces) taco seasoning mix
2 tablespoons *Frank's® RedHot® Original Cayenne Pepper Sauce*
1 egg, beaten
4 flour tortillas (10 inches)
¹⁄₃ cup sour cream
½ cup (2 ounces) shredded Cheddar cheese

·39·

Filled & Skewered

Sesame Italian Breadsticks

¼ cup grated Parmesan
    cheese
3 tablespoons sesame seeds
2 teaspoons dried Italian
    seasoning
1 teaspoon kosher salt
    (optional)
12 frozen bread dough
    dinner rolls, thawed
¼ cup butter, melted

1. Preheat oven to 425°F. Spray large baking sheet with nonstick cooking spray.

2. Combine cheese, sesame seeds, Italian seasoning and salt, if desired, in small bowl. Spread out on plate.

3. Roll each dinner roll into rope, about 8 inches long and ½ inch thick, on lightly floured surface; place on baking sheet. Brush tops and sides with butter. Roll each buttered rope in cheese mixture, pressing mixture into dough. Return ropes to baking sheet, placing 2 inches apart. Twist each rope 3 times. Press both ends of rope down on baking sheet. Bake 10 to 12 minutes or until golden brown.

Makes 12 breadsticks

Filled & Skewered

Spinach Cheese Bundles

1. Preheat oven to 400°F. Combine cheese, spinach and pepper in small bowl; mix well.

2. Roll out 1 sheet puff pastry on floured surface into 12-inch square. Cut into 16 (3-inch) squares. Place about 1 teaspoon cheese mixture in center of each square. Brush edges of squares with water. Bring edges together over filling; twist tightly to seal. Fan out corners of puff pastry.

3. Place bundles 2 inches apart on ungreased baking sheet. Bake about 13 minutes or until golden brown. Repeat with remaining sheets of puff pastry and cheese mixture. Serve warm with dipping sauce, if desired.

Makes 32 bundles

1 package (6½ ounces) garlic-and-herb spreadable cheese
½ cup chopped fresh spinach
¼ teaspoon black pepper
1 package (17¼ ounces) frozen puff pastry, thawed
Sweet-and-sour or favorite dipping sauce (optional)

¼ cup creamy peanut
butter
2 tablespoons finely
chopped onion
2 tablespoons finely
chopped parsley
2 tablespoons fresh lemon
juice
1½ teaspoons soy sauce
1 clove garlic, finely
chopped
1 teaspoon TABASCO®
brand Pepper Sauce
½ teaspoon ground
coriander
1 pound boneless, skinless
chicken breasts, cut
into 1-inch pieces
Wooden skewers

Filled & Skewered

Thai Chicken Skewers

Combine all ingredients except chicken and skewers in medium bowl. Add chicken; toss to coat. Cover and refrigerate 6 to 8 hours or overnight.

Preheat broiler or grill. Thread marinated chicken on skewers.

Broil or grill 6 to 8 minutes, turning frequently. (Do not overcook.) Serve warm on skewers.

Makes 30 to 35 pieces

Party Chicken Tarts

Melt 2 tablespoons butter in large skillet until hot. Add mushrooms, celery and onion; cook and stir 4 to 5 minutes. Sprinkle with flour; stir in chicken and sour cream. Cook until thoroughly heated. Stir in garlic salt; set aside.

Cut each biscuit into quarters; press each piece into miniature muffin tin coated with cooking spray to form tart shell. Brush each piece with melted butter. Bake at 400°F 6 minutes. Remove from oven; reduce oven temperature to 350°F.

Fill each tart with 1 teaspoon chicken mixture; sprinkle with cheese. Bake 14 to 15 minutes more. Serve immediately.   *Makes 40 to 48 appetizers*

Note: For ease in serving at party time, prepare filling ahead of time and cook tarts 5 minutes. Fill and bake just before serving for best flavor.

Favorite recipe from **National Chicken Council**

1½ cups chopped cooked chicken
2 tablespoons butter or margarine
1 cup chopped fresh mushrooms
¼ cup finely chopped celery
¼ cup finely chopped onion
2 tablespoons all-purpose flour
6 tablespoons sour cream
½ teaspoon garlic salt
1 package (10 ounces) flaky refrigerator biscuits (10 to 12 count)
Vegetable cooking spray
1 tablespoon butter or margarine, melted
Grated Parmesan cheese

Filled & Skewered

½ package (17¼ ounces) frozen puff pastry, thawed

1 tablespoon Dijon mustard

½ cup (2 ounces) finely shredded Cheddar cheese

1 teaspoon black pepper

1 egg

1 tablespoon water

Pepper Cheese Cocktail Puffs

1. Preheat oven to 400°F. Grease baking sheets.

2. Roll out 1 sheet puff pastry dough on well floured surface to 14×10-inch rectangle. Spread half of dough (from 10-inch side) with mustard. Sprinkle with cheese and pepper. Fold dough over filling; roll gently to seal edges. Cut lengthwise into 3 strips; cut each strip diagonally into 1½-inch pieces. Place on prepared baking sheets. Beat egg and water in small bowl; brush onto appetizers.

3. Bake appetizers 12 to 15 minutes or until puffed and deep golden brown. Remove from baking sheet to wire rack; cool.   *Makes about 20 appetizers*

Tip: Work quickly and efficiently when using puff pastry. The colder the puff pastry, the better it will puff in the hot oven.

Filled & Skewered

Spicy Orange Chicken Kabob Appetizers

1. Cut chicken and bell pepper into 24 (¾-inch) square pieces. Place chicken, pepper and mushrooms in large resealable plastic food storage bag. Combine orange juice, soy sauce, oil, onion powder and five-spice powder in small bowl. Pour over chicken and vegetables. Seal bag securely; turn to coat. Marinate in refrigerator 4 to 24 hours, turning frequently.

2. Soak 24 small wooden skewers or toothpicks in water 20 minutes. Meanwhile, preheat broiler. Coat broiler pan with nonstick cooking spray.

3. Drain chicken mixture, reserving marinade. Thread 1 piece chicken, 1 piece pepper and 1 mushroom onto each skewer. Place on prepared pan. Brush with marinade; discard remaining marinade. Broil kabobs 4 inches from heat 5 to 6 minutes or until chicken is no longer pink in center. Serve immediately.

Makes 12 servings

Chinese five-spice powder is a blend of cinnamon, cloves, fennel seed, anise and Szechuan peppercorns. It is available in most supermarkets and at Asian grocery stores.

2 boneless skinless chicken breasts (about 8 ounces)
1 small red or green bell pepper
24 small fresh button mushrooms
½ cup orange juice
2 tablespoons soy sauce
1 tablespoon vegetable oil
1½ teaspoons onion powder
½ teaspoon Chinese five-spice powder*

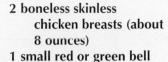

Spiced Sesame Wonton Crisps

20 (3-inch) wonton
 wrappers, cut in half
1 tablespoon water
2 teaspoons olive oil
½ teaspoon paprika
½ teaspoon ground cumin
 or chili powder
¼ teaspoon dry mustard
1 tablespoon sesame seeds

1. Preheat oven to 375°F. Coat 2 large nonstick baking sheets with nonstick cooking spray. Cut each halved wonton wrapper into 2 strips; place in single layer on prepared baking sheets.

2. Combine water, oil, paprika, cumin and mustard in small bowl; mix well. Brush oil mixture onto wonton strips; sprinkle with sesame seeds.

3. Bake 6 to 8 minutes or until lightly browned. Remove to wire rack; cool completely. Transfer to serving plate. *Makes 8 servings*

Filled & Skewered

Grilled Spiced Halibut, Pineapple and Pepper Skewers

1. Combine lemon juice, chili powder, garlic, cumin, cinnamon and cloves in large resealable plastic food storage bag; knead until blended.

2. Rinse fish; pat dry. Cut into 12 (1- to 1¼-inch-square) cubes. Add fish to bag. Press out air; seal. Turn gently to coat fish with marinade. Refrigerate 30 minutes to 1 hour. Soak 12 (6- to 8-inch) bamboo skewers in water while fish marinates. Alternately thread 2 pieces pineapple, 2 pieces bell pepper and 1 piece fish onto each skewer.

3. Spray cold grid with nonstick cooking spray. Adjust grid 4 to 6 inches above heat. Preheat grill to medium-high heat. Place skewers on grill. Cover, if possible (or tent with foil); grill 3 to 4 minutes or until grill marks appear on bottom. Turn skewers over; grill 3 to 4 minutes more or until fish is opaque and flakes easily when tested with fork. *Makes 6 servings*

2 tablespoons lemon juice
   or lime juice
1 teaspoon chili powder
1 teaspoon minced garlic
½ teaspoon ground cumin
¼ teaspoon ground
   cinnamon
⅛ teaspoon ground cloves
½ pound boneless skinless
   halibut steak, about
   1 inch thick
½ small pineapple, peeled,
   halved lengthwise and
   cut into 24 pieces
1 large green or red bell
   pepper, cut into
   24 pieces

Filled & Skewered

1 tablespoon vegetable oil
½ cup chopped onion
½ cup chopped red bell pepper
2 cups chopped cooked chicken
⅔ cup prepared sweet-and-sour sauce
½ cup chopped almonds
2 tablespoons soy sauce
6 (6- or 7-inch) flour tortillas

Almond Chicken Cups

1. Preheat oven to 400°F. Heat oil in small skillet over medium heat until hot. Add onion and bell pepper; cook and stir 3 minutes or until crisp-tender.

2. Combine vegetable mixture, chicken, sweet-and-sour sauce, almonds and soy sauce in medium bowl; mix until well blended.

3. Cut each tortilla in half. Place each half in 2¾-inch muffin cup. Fill each with about ¼ cup chicken mixture. Bake 8 to 10 minutes or until tortilla edges are crisp and filling is hot. Remove muffin pan to wire rack. Let stand 5 minutes before serving. *Makes 12 chicken cups*

Party Stuffed Pinwheels

1. Preheat oven to 425°F. In medium bowl, combine all ingredients except pizza crusts; set aside.

2. Unroll pizza crusts, then top evenly with filling. Roll, starting at longest side, jelly-roll style. Cut into 32 rounds.**

3. On baking sheet sprayed with nonstick cooking spray, arrange rounds cut side down. Bake, uncovered, 13 minutes or until golden brown.

Makes 32 pinwheels

Also terrific with LIPTON® RECIPE SECRETS® Onion Soup Mix.

**If rolled pizza crust is too soft to cut, refrigerate or freeze until firm.*

1 envelope LIPTON®
RECIPE SECRETS®
Savory Herb with
Garlic Soup Mix*
1 package (8 ounces)
cream cheese, softened
1 cup shredded mozzarella
cheese (about
4 ounces)
2 tablespoons milk
1 tablespoon grated
Parmesan cheese
2 packages (10 ounces
each) refrigerated
pizza crust

Filled & Skewered

1 teaspoon vegetable oil
½ cup chopped onion
½ cup chopped green bell pepper
¼ teaspoon salt
⅛ teaspoon dried basil leaves
⅛ teaspoon dried oregano leaves
⅛ teaspoon black pepper
1 can (12 ounces) country biscuits (10 biscuits)
¼ cup (1 ounce) shredded mozzarella cheese
½ cup prepared spaghetti or pizza sauce
2 tablespoons grated Parmesan cheese

Filled & Showered

Onion and Pepper Calzones

1. Preheat oven to 400°F. Heat oil in medium nonstick skillet over medium-high heat. Add onion and bell pepper; cook 5 minutes, stirring occasionally. Remove from heat. Add salt, basil, oregano and black pepper; stir to combine. Remove from heat; cool slightly. Meanwhile, flatten biscuits into 3½-inch circles about ⅛ inch thick.

2. Stir mozzarella cheese into onion mixture. Spoon 1 teaspoon onion mixture onto each biscuit. Fold biscuits in half, covering filling. Press edges with tines of fork to seal; transfer to baking sheet. Bake 10 to 12 minutes or until golden brown. While calzones are baking, place spaghetti sauce in small microwavable bowl. Cover with vented plastic wrap. Microwave at HIGH 3 minutes or until hot.

3. To serve, spoon spaghetti sauce and Parmesan cheese over each calzone. Serve immediately. *Makes 10 appetizers*

Chicken Kabobs with Thai Dipping Sauce

Thread chicken, cucumber, tomatoes and onions alternately onto metal skewers; set aside.

To prepare Thai Dipping Sauce, combine teriyaki baste & glaze sauce, **Frank's RedHot** Sauce, peanut butter, orange juice concentrate and garlic; mix well. Reserve ⅔ cup sauce for dipping.

Brush skewers with some of remaining sauce. Place skewers on oiled grid. Grill over hot coals 10 minutes or until chicken is no longer pink in center, turning and basting often with remaining sauce. Serve skewers with reserved Thai Dipping Sauce. Garnish as desired.   *Makes 6 appetizer servings*

Prep Time: *15 minutes*
Cook Time: *10 minutes*

1 pound boneless skinless chicken breasts, cut into 1-inch cubes
1 small cucumber, seeded and cut into small chunks
1 cup cherry tomatoes
2 green onions, cut into 1-inch pieces
⅔ cup teriyaki baste & glaze sauce
⅓ cup *Frank's® RedHot®* Original Cayenne Pepper Sauce
⅓ cup peanut butter
3 tablespoons frozen orange juice concentrate, undiluted
2 cloves garlic, minced

Pizza Snack Cups

1 can (12 ounces)
    refrigerated biscuits
    (10 biscuits)
½ pound ground beef
1 jar (14 ounces) RAGÚ®
    Pizza Quick® Sauce
½ cup shredded mozzarella
    cheese (about
    2 ounces)

1. Preheat oven to 375°F. In muffin pan, evenly press each biscuit into bottom and up side of each cup; chill until ready to fill.

2. In 10-inch skillet, brown ground beef over medium-high heat; drain. Stir in Ragú Pizza Quick Sauce and heat through.

3. Evenly spoon beef mixture into prepared muffin cups. Bake 15 minutes. Sprinkle with cheese and bake an additional 5 minutes or until cheese is melted and biscuits are golden. Let stand 5 minutes. Gently remove pizza cups from muffin pan and serve. *Makes 10 pizza cups*

Prep Time: *10 minutes*
Cook Time: *25 minutes*

Filled & Skewered

Tortellini Kabobs with Pesto Ranch Dip

1. Cook tortellini according to package directions. Rinse and drain under cold water. Thread tortellini onto bamboo skewers, 2 tortellini per skewer.

2. Combine salad dressing, cheese, garlic and basil in small bowl.

3. Serve tortellini kabobs with dip.   *Makes 6 to 8 servings*

Serving suggestion: For an even quicker dip, combine purchased spaghetti sauce or salsa with some finely chopped black olives.

½ (16-ounce) bag frozen tortellini
1¼ cups prepared ranch salad dressing
½ cup grated Parmesan cheese
3 cloves garlic, minced
2 teaspoons dried basil leaves

Filled & Skewered

Top These!

Arizona Cheese Crisp

Vegetable oil for deep-frying
2 (10- or 12-inch) flour tortillas
1 to 1½ cups (4 to 6 ounces) shredded Cheddar or Monterey Jack cheese
½ cup picante sauce
¼ cup grated Parmesan cheese

1. Pour oil into wok to depth of 1 inch. Place over medium-high heat until oil registers 360°F on deep-frying thermometer. Slide 1 tortilla into oil. Using 2 slotted spoons, gently hold center of tortilla down so oil flows over edges. When tortilla is crisp and golden on bottom, carefully tilt wok, holding tortilla in place with spoon, to cover edge of tortilla with oil; cook until lightly browned. Rotate tortilla as needed to lightly brown entire edge. Remove from oil; drain on paper towels, curled side down. Repeat with second tortilla. Cover loosely; let stand at room temperature. (Tortillas can be made up to 8 hours in advance.)

2. Preheat oven to 350°F. Place shells, curled side up, on baking sheet. Sprinkle each with Cheddar cheese; top with picante sauce. Sprinkle with Parmesan cheese.

3. Bake, uncovered, 8 to 10 minutes or until cheeses melt. To serve, break into bite-size pieces. *Makes 4 to 6 servings*

Chorizo Cheese Crisp: Remove casing from ¼ pound chorizo sausage. Crumble sausage into large skillet; stir over medium-high heat until browned. Drain fat. Follow directions for Arizona Cheese Crisp, substituting chorizo for Parmesan cheese.

Olive Cheese Crisp: Follow directions for Arizona Cheese Crisp, omitting picante sauce and Parmesan cheese. Sprinkle ⅓ cup sliced pitted ripe olives and ⅓ cup diced green chilies over Cheddar cheese.

Southwestern Potato Skins Olé

6 large baking potatoes, scrubbed
¾ pound ground beef
⅔ cup water
1 package (1¼ ounces) taco seasoning
½ cup sliced green onions
1 tomato, chopped
1 can (2¼ ounces) sliced black olives, drained
1 cup (4 ounces) shredded Cheddar cheese
2 cups Quick Taco Dip (recipe follows)

1. Pierce potatoes with fork. Microwave at HIGH 30 minutes, turning over after 15 minutes; let cool. Cut potatoes in half; scoop out insides, leaving ¼-inch-thick shell. Reserve potato insides for another use.

2. Cook and stir ground beef in large skillet over medium-high heat until crumbly and no longer pink. Drain. Stir in water and taco seasoning; bring to a boil. Reduce heat to low; cook, uncovered, 15 minutes. Stir in green onions. Preheat broiler.

3. Spoon meat mixture into potato shells; top with tomato, olives and cheese. Place filled potato shells on baking sheet; heat under broiler until cheese is melted. Top with Quick Taco Dip. *Makes 6 servings*

Quick Taco Dip: Combine 2 cups sour cream and 1 package (1¼ ounces) taco seasoning in medium bowl; mix well. Refrigerate until ready to serve. Makes 2 cups.

Top These!

Mushroom Parmesan Crostini

Preheat oven to 375°F. In 8-inch nonstick skillet, heat olive oil over medium heat and cook garlic 30 seconds. Add mushrooms and cook, stirring occasionally, 2 minutes or until liquid evaporates.

On baking sheet, arrange bread slices. Evenly spread Ragú Pizza Quick Sauce on bread slices, then top with mushroom mixture, cheese and basil.

Bake 15 minutes or until heated through. *Makes 12 crostini*

Tip: Many varieties of mushrooms are available in supermarkets and specialty grocery stores. Shiitake, portobello and cremini mushrooms all lend delicious flavors.

1 tablespoon olive oil

1 clove garlic, finely chopped

1 cup chopped mushrooms

1 loaf Italian or French bread (about 12 inches long), cut into 12 slices and toasted

¾ cup RAGÚ® Pizza Quick® Sauce

¼ cup grated Parmesan cheese

1 tablespoon finely chopped fresh basil leaves or 1 teaspoon dried basil leaves

•57•
Top These!

Shrimp Toast

½ pound raw shrimp, peeled and deveined
2 tablespoons chopped green onion
2 tablespoons finely chopped water chestnuts
2 tablespoons soy sauce
1 teaspoon dark sesame oil
1 egg white, lightly beaten
6 slices white sandwich bread, crusts removed
Red and yellow bell pepper, for garnish

1. Finely chop shrimp, or place in food processor container. Cover; process, using on/off pulses, about 10 times or until shrimp are finely chopped. Combine shrimp, onion, water chestnuts, soy sauce and sesame oil in medium bowl; mix well. Stir in egg white; mix well.*

2. Toast bread lightly on both sides. Cut diagonally into quarters. Spread shrimp mixture evenly over toast to edges.

3. Place toast on foil-lined baking sheet or broiler pan. Broil 6 inches from heat 4 to 5 minutes or until lightly browned. Garnish with peppers.

Makes 2 dozen appetizers

The filling may be made ahead to this point. Cover and refrigerate filling up to 24 hours. Proceed as directed in step 3.

Top These!

Picnic Pizza Biscuits

1. Preheat oven to 375°F. Separate biscuits; pat or roll into 10 (4-inch) circles on floured surface. Press circles into 12-cup muffin pan.

2. Cook sausage in large nonstick skillet over high heat 5 minutes or until browned, stirring to separate meat; drain fat. Add onion, mushrooms and bell pepper; cook and stir 3 minutes or until vegetables are tender. Stir in cheese, sauce and mustard; mix well.

3. Mound filling evenly in biscuits. Bake 20 minutes or until biscuits are browned. Serve warm or at room temperature.   *Makes 10 servings*

Prep Time: *30 minutes*
Cook Time: *25 minutes*

1 can (10 ounces) refrigerated buttermilk biscuits
1 pound hot Italian sausage, casings removed
½ cup chopped onion
½ cup sliced mushrooms
½ cup chopped green bell pepper
½ cup (2 ounces) shredded mozzarella cheese
¼ cup marinara or pizza sauce
2 tablespoons *French's®* Honey Dijon Mustard

Top These!

Reuben Bites

24 party rye bread slices
½ cup prepared Thousand
  Island dressing
6 ounces turkey pastrami,
  very thinly sliced
1 cup (4 ounces) shredded
  Swiss cheese
1 cup alfalfa sprouts

1. Preheat oven to 400°F.

2. Arrange bread slices on nonstick baking sheet. Bake 5 minutes or until lightly toasted.

3. Spread 1 teaspoon dressing onto each bread slice; top with pastrami, folding to fit bread slices. Sprinkle evenly with cheese. Bake 5 minutes or until hot. Top with sprouts. Transfer to serving plate. *Makes 12 servings*

Top These!

Carpaccio di Zucchini

1. Preheat broiler. Place zucchini in medium bowl. Add almonds and dressing; mix well. Set aside.

2. Place baguette halves on large baking sheet; spread evenly with margarine. Sprinkle with cheese. Broil 3 inches from heat 2 to 3 minutes or until edges and cheese are browned.

3. Spread zucchini mixture evenly onto each baguette half. Serve immediately.

Makes 4 servings

Serving Suggestion: Serve with spaghetti with tomato sauce.

¾ **pound zucchini, shredded**
½ **cup sliced almonds, toasted**
1 **tablespoon prepared Italian dressing**
4 **French bread baguettes, sliced in half lengthwise**
1 **tablespoon plus 1 teaspoon soft-spread margarine**
3 **tablespoons grated Parmesan cheese**

Top These!

Sweet Pepper Pizza Fingers

2 tablespoons margarine or butter

2 large red, green and/or yellow bell peppers, thinly sliced

1 clove garlic, finely chopped

1 envelope LIPTON® RECIPE SECRETS® Onion Soup Mix

1 cup water

1 package (10 ounces) refrigerated pizza crust

1½ cups shredded mozzarella cheese (about 6 ounces), divided

Preheat oven to 425°F.

In 12-inch skillet, melt margarine over medium heat; cook peppers and garlic, stirring occasionally, 5 minutes or until peppers are tender. Stir in soup mix blended with water. Bring to a boil over high heat. Reduce heat to low and simmer uncovered 6 minutes or until liquid is absorbed. Remove from heat; set aside to cool 5 minutes.

Meanwhile, on baking sheet sprayed with nonstick cooking spray, roll out pizza crust into 12×8-inch rectangle. Sprinkle 1 cup mozzarella cheese over crust; top with cooked pepper mixture, spreading to edges of dough. Top with remaining ½ cup mozzarella cheese. Bake 10 minutes or until crust is golden brown and topping is bubbly. Remove from oven and let stand 5 minutes. To serve, cut into 4×1-inch strips.

Makes about 24 appetizers

Top These!

Quattro Formaggio Pizza

1. Heat oven to 450°F.

2. Place bread shell on baking sheet. Spread pizza sauce evenly over bread shell. Top with provolone, mozzarella, Asiago and Parmesan cheeses.

3. Bake 14 minutes or until bread shell is golden brown and cheese is melted. Cut into wedges; serve immediately. *Makes 8 servings*

1 (12-inch) Italian bread shell

½ cup prepared pizza or marinara sauce

4 ounces shaved or thinly sliced provolone cheese

1 cup (4 ounces) shredded smoked or regular mozzarella cheese

2 ounces Asiago or brick cheese, thinly sliced

¼ cup freshly grated Parmesan or Romano cheese

Top These!

Fast Pesto Focaccia

1 can (10 ounces)
    refrigerated pizza crust
    dough
2 tablespoons prepared
    pesto
4 sun-dried tomatoes
    (packed in oil), drained

1. Preheat oven to 425°F. Lightly grease 8×8×2-inch pan. Unroll pizza dough. Fold in half; pat into pan.

2. Spread pesto evenly over dough. Chop tomatoes or snip with kitchen scissors; sprinkle over pesto. Press tomatoes into dough. Using wooden spoon handle, make indentations in dough every 2 inches .

3. Bake 10 to 12 minutes or until golden brown. Cut into 16 squares; serve warm or at room temperature.

Makes 16 servings

Top These!

Mediterranean Pita Pizzas

1. Preheat oven to 450°F.

2. Arrange pita rounds on baking sheet; brush tops with oil. Bake 6 minutes.

3. Meanwhile, place beans in small bowl; mash lightly with fork. Stir in lemon juice and garlic. Spread bean mixture evenly onto pita rounds to within ½ inch of edge. Arrange remaining ingredients evenly on pitas. Bake 5 minutes or until topping is thoroughly heated and crust is crisp. Cut into quarters. Serve hot.

Makes 8 servings

2 (8-inch) pita bread rounds
1 cup rinsed and drained canned cannellini beans
2 teaspoons lemon juice
2 medium cloves garlic, minced
1 teaspoon olive oil
½ cup thinly sliced radicchio or escarole lettuce (optional)
½ cup chopped seeded tomato
½ cup finely chopped red onion
¼ cup (1 ounce) crumbled feta cheese
2 tablespoons thinly sliced pitted black olives

Top These!

Cheesy Potato Skins with Black Beans & Salsa

6 medium potatoes
   (6 ounces each), baked
¾ cup GUILTLESS
   GOURMET® Black
   Bean Dip (Spicy or
   Mild)
¾ cup (3 ounces) grated
   Cheddar cheese
¾ cup GUILTLESS
   GOURMET® Salsa
   (Roasted Red Pepper
   or Southwestern Grill)
¾ cup low fat sour cream
   Fresh cilantro sprigs
   (optional)

Preheat oven to 400°F. Cut baked potatoes in half lengthwise and scoop out potato pulp, leaving ¼ inch pulp attached to skin (avoid breaking skin). (Save potato pulp for another use, such as mashed potatoes.) Place potato skins on large baking sheet, skin sides down; bake 5 minutes.

Fill each potato skin with 1 tablespoon bean dip and 1 tablespoon cheese. Return to oven; bake 10 minutes.

Remove from oven; let cool 5 minutes. Dollop 1 tablespoon salsa and 1 tablespoon sour cream onto each potato. Garnish with cilantro, if desired. Serve hot.

Makes 12 servings

Top These!

Pepperoni-Oregano Focaccia

1. Preheat oven to 425°F. Grease large baking sheet; sprinkle with cornmeal. Set aside.

2. Unroll dough onto lightly floured surface. Pat dough into 12×9-inch rectangle. Sprinkle half the pepperoni and half the oregano over one side of dough. Fold over dough, making 12×4½-inch rectangle. Roll dough into 12×9-inch rectangle. Place on prepared baking sheet. Prick dough with fork at 2-inch intervals about 30 times. Brush with oil; sprinkle with remaining pepperoni and oregano.

3. Bake 12 to 15 minutes or until golden brown. (Prick dough several more times if dough puffs as it bakes.) Cut into strips.   *Makes 12 servings*

1 tablespoon cornmeal
1 can (10 ounces) refrigerated pizza crust dough
½ cup finely chopped pepperoni (3 to 3½ ounces)
1½ teaspoons finely chopped fresh oregano *or* ½ teaspoon dried oregano leaves
2 teaspoons olive oil

Top These!

Artichoke Crostini

1 jar (6 ounces) marinated artichoke hearts, drained and chopped
3 green onions, chopped
5 tablespoons grated Parmesan cheese, divided
2 tablespoons mayonnaise
12 slices French bread (½ inch thick)

1. Preheat broiler. Combine artichokes, green onions, 3 tablespoons cheese and mayonnaise in small bowl; mix well. Set aside.

2. Arrange bread slices on baking sheet. Broil 4 to 5 inches from heat 2 to 3 minutes on each side or until lightly browned.

3. Spoon about 1 tablespoon artichoke mixture onto each bread slice; sprinkle with remaining 2 tablespoons cheese. Broil 1 to 2 minutes or until cheese is melted and lightly browned. *Makes 4 servings*

Tip: Garnish crostini with red bell pepper, if desired.

Top These!

Cheese and Pepper Stuffed Potato Skins

1. Preheat oven to 450°F. Wrap potatoes in foil; bake about 1 hour 15 minutes or until fork-tender. Let stand until cool enough to handle. Cut each potato in half lengthwise; scoop out insides,* leaving a ¼-inch-thick shell. Cut shells in half crosswise. Place shells on large baking sheet.

2. Preheat broiler. Combine 1 tablespoon **Frank's RedHot** Sauce and butter in small bowl; brush onto inside of each potato shell. Broil shells, 6 inches from heat, 8 minutes or until golden brown and crispy.

3. Combine remaining 3 tablespoons **Frank's RedHot** Sauce with remaining ingredients in large bowl. Spoon about 2 tablespoons mixture into each potato shell. Broil 2 minutes or until cheese melts. Cut each piece in half to serve.

Makes 12 servings

Reserve leftover potato for mashed potatoes, home-fries or soup.

Prep Time: *30 minutes*
Cook Time: *1 hour 20 minutes*

6 large russet potatoes (about ¾ pound each), scrubbed
4 tablespoons *Frank's® RedHot®* Original Cayenne Pepper Sauce, divided
2 tablespoons butter, melted
1 large red bell pepper, seeded and finely chopped
1 cup chopped green onions
1 cup (4 ounces) shredded Cheddar cheese

Top These!

Bruschetta

Nonstick cooking spray
1 cup thinly sliced onion (about 1 large)
½ cup chopped seeded tomato
2 tablespoons capers
¼ teaspoon black pepper
3 cloves garlic, finely chopped
1 teaspoon olive oil
4 slices French bread
½ cup (2 ounces) shredded reduced-fat Monterey Jack cheese

1. Spray large nonstick skillet with cooking spray. Heat over medium heat until hot. Add onion; cook and stir 5 minutes. Stir in tomato, capers and pepper. Cook 3 minutes.

2. Preheat broiler.

3. Combine garlic and oil in small bowl. Brush bread slices with mixture. Top with onion mixture; sprinkle with cheese. Place on baking sheet. Broil 3 minutes or until cheese melts. *Makes 4 servings*

Top These!

Chicken Pesto Pizza

1. Preheat oven to 375°F. Sprinkle baking sheet with cornmeal. Roll out bread dough on floured surface to 14×8-inch rectangle. Transfer to prepared baking sheet. Cover loosely with plastic wrap; let rise 20 to 30 minutes.

2. Meanwhile, spray large skillet with cooking spray; heat over medium heat. Add chicken; cook and stir 2 minutes. Add onion and pesto; cook and stir 3 to 4 minutes or until chicken is cooked through. Stir in tomatoes. Remove from heat; let cool slightly.

3. Spread chicken mixture evenly over bread dough within 1 inch of edges. Sprinkle with cheese. Bake on bottom rack of oven about 20 minutes or until crust is golden brown. Cut into 2-inch squares.   *Makes about 20 pieces*

Cornmeal
1 loaf (1 pound) frozen
   bread dough, thawed
   Nonstick cooking spray
8 ounces chicken tenders,
   cut into ½-inch pieces
½ red onion, cut into
   quarters and thinly
   sliced
¼ cup prepared pesto
2 large plum tomatoes,
   seeded and diced
1 cup (4 ounces) shredded
   pizza cheese blend or
   mozzarella cheese

Top These!

Cheddar Tomato Bacon Toasts

1 jar (1 pound) RAGÚ®
   Cheese Creations!®
   Double Cheddar Sauce
1 medium tomato, chopped
5 slices bacon, crisp-cooked
   and crumbled (about
   ⅓ cup)
2 loaves Italian bread (each
   about 16 inches long),
   each cut into 16 slices

1. Preheat oven to 350°F. In medium bowl, combine Ragú Cheese Creations! Sauce, tomato and bacon.

2. On baking sheet, arrange bread slices. Evenly top with sauce mixture.

3. Bake 10 minutes or until sauce mixture is bubbling. Serve immediately.

Makes 16 servings

Prep Time: *10 minutes*
Cook Time: *10 minutes*

Top These!

Tortilla Pizzettes

1. Pour salsa into strainer; let drain at least 20 minutes.

2. Meanwhile, combine refried beans, cilantro and cumin in small bowl; mix well. Preheat oven to 400°F. Spray baking sheet lightly with nonstick cooking spray; set aside.

3. Cut each tortilla into 2½-inch circles with round cookie cutter (9 to 10 circles per tortilla). Spread each tortilla circle with refried bean mixture, leaving ¼ inch around edge. Top each with heaping teaspoonful drained salsa; sprinkle with about 1½ teaspoons cheese. Place pizzettes on prepared baking sheet. Bake about 7 minutes or until tortillas are golden brown.

Makes about 30 pizzettes

1 cup chunky salsa
1 cup refried beans
2 tablespoons chopped
 fresh cilantro
½ teaspoon ground cumin
3 (10-inch) flour tortillas
1 cup (4 ounces) shredded
 Mexican cheese blend

•73•

Top These!

Wings & Things

Nicole's Cheddar Crisps

1¾ cups all-purpose flour
½ cup yellow cornmeal
¾ teaspoon sugar
¾ teaspoon salt
½ teaspoon baking soda
½ cup (1 stick) butter or margarine
1½ cups (6 ounces) shredded sharp Cheddar cheese
½ cup cold water
2 tablespoons white vinegar
Coarsely ground black pepper

1. Mix flour, cornmeal, sugar, salt and baking soda in large bowl. Cut in butter with pastry blender or two knives until mixture resembles coarse crumbs. Stir in cheese, water and vinegar with fork until mixture forms soft dough. Cover dough; refrigerate 1 hour or freeze 30 minutes until firm.

2. Preheat oven to 375°F. Grease 2 large cookie sheets. Divide dough into 4 pieces. Roll each piece into paper-thin circle (about 13 inches in diameter) on floured surface. Sprinkle with pepper; press pepper firmly into dough.

3. Cut each circle into 8 wedges; place on prepared cookie sheets. Bake about 10 minutes or until crisp. Store in airtight container for up to 3 days.

Makes 32 crisps

Magic Fried Oysters

6 dozen medium to large shucked oysters in their liquor (about 3 pounds)

3 tablespoons Chef Paul Prudhomme's Seafood Magic®

1 cup all-purpose flour

1 cup corn flour

1 cup cornmeal
Vegetable oil for deep-frying

Place oysters and oyster liquor in large bowl. Add 2 tablespoons of the Seafood Magic® to oysters, stirring well. In medium bowl, combine flour, corn flour, cornmeal and the remaining Seafood Magic®.

Heat 2 inches or more of oil in deep-fryer or large saucepan to 375°F. Drain oysters and then use a slotted spoon to toss them lightly and quickly in seasoned flour mixture (so oysters don't produce excess moisture, which cakes the flour). Shake off excess flour and carefully slip each oyster into hot oil.

Fry in single layer in batches just until crispy and golden brown, 1 to 1½ minutes; do not overcook. (Adjust heat as needed to maintain temperature at about 375°F.) Drain on paper towels and serve.   *Makes 6 servings*

Buffalo Chicken Wings

Cut tips off wings at first joint; discard tips. Cut remaining wings into two parts at the joint; sprinkle with salt and pepper.

Heat oil in deep fryer or heavy saucepan to 375°F. Add half the wings; fry about 10 minutes or until golden brown and crisp, stirring occasionally. Remove with slotted spoon; drain on paper towels. Repeat with remaining wings.

Melt butter in small saucepan over medium heat; stir in pepper sauce and vinegar. Cook until thoroughly heated. Place wings on large platter. Pour sauce over wings. Serve warm with celery and dressing for dipping.

Makes 24 appetizers

*Favorite recipe from **National Chicken Council***

24 chicken wings
1 teaspoon salt
¼ teaspoon ground black pepper
4 cups vegetable oil for frying
¼ cup butter or margarine
¼ cup hot pepper sauce
1 teaspoon white wine vinegar
Celery sticks
1 bottle (8 ounces) blue cheese dressing

Smoked Chicken Bagel Snacks

1. Combine cream cheese and mustard in small bowl; mix well.

2. Stir in peppers and green onion.

3. Spread cream cheese mixture evenly onto cut sides of bagels. Cover bottom halves of bagels with chicken, folding chicken to fit onto bagels. Top with cucumber slices and bagel tops.   *Makes 5 servings*

⅓ cup fat-free cream cheese, softened

2 teaspoons spicy brown mustard

¼ cup chopped roasted red peppers

1 green onion with top, sliced

5 mini-bagels, split

3 ounces smoked chicken or turkey, cut into 10 very thin slices

¼ medium cucumber, cut into 10 thin slices

Wings & Things

Tortilla Crunch Chicken Fingers

1. Preheat oven to 400°F.

2. In medium bowl, combine savory herb with garlic soup mix and tortilla chips. In large plastic bag or bowl, combine chicken and egg beaten with water until evenly coated. Remove chicken and dip in tortilla mixture until evenly coated; discard bag. On 15½×10½×1-inch jelly-roll pan sprayed with nonstick cooking spray, arrange chicken; drizzle with I Can't Believe It's Not Butter!® Spread.

3. Bake, uncovered, 12 minutes or until chicken is thoroughly cooked. Serve with chunky salsa, if desired.   *Makes about 24 chicken fingers*

- 1 envelope LIPTON® RECIPE SECRETS® Savory Herb with Garlic Soup Mix
- 1 cup finely crushed plain tortilla chips or cornflakes (about 3 ounces)
- 1½ pounds boneless, skinless chicken breasts, cut into strips
- 1 egg
- 2 tablespoons water
- 2 tablespoons I CAN'T BELIEVE IT'S NOT BUTTER!® Spread, melted

Wings & Things

Spanish Omelet

8 large eggs, beaten
3 cups (16 ounces) frozen cubed or shredded hash brown potatoes
1½ cups *French's®* French Fried Onions
Salsa
Frank's® RedHot® Original Cayenne Pepper Sauce

1. Beat eggs with ½ *teaspoon salt* and ¼ *teaspoon pepper* in large bowl; set aside.

2. Heat *2 tablespoons oil* until very hot in 10-inch nonstick oven-safe skillet over medium-high heat. Sauté potatoes about 7 minutes or until browned, stirring often.

3. Stir ½ *cup* French Fried Onions and beaten eggs into potato mixture. Cook, uncovered, over low heat 15 minutes or until eggs are almost set. *Do not stir.* Sprinkle eggs with remaining *1 cup* onions. Cover and cook 8 minutes or until eggs are fully set. Cut into wedges and serve with salsa. Splash on *Frank's RedHot* Sauce to taste.

Makes 6 servings

Prep Time: *5 minutes*
Cook Time: *30 minutes*

Buffalo Chicken Wing Sampler

2½ pounds chicken wing pieces
½ cup *Frank's® RedHot®* Original Cayenne Pepper Sauce
⅓ cup melted butter

1. Deep-fry* wings in hot oil (400°F) for 12 minutes until fully cooked and crispy; drain.

2. Combine **Frank's RedHot** Sauce and butter. Dip wings in sauce to coat.

3. Serve wings with celery and blue cheese dressing if desired.

Makes 8 appetizer servings

For equally crispy wings, bake 1 hour at 425°F, or grill 30 minutes over medium heat.

RedHot Sampler Variations: Add one of the following to **RedHot** butter mixture; heat through. Tex-Mex: 1 tablespoon chili powder, ¼ teaspoon garlic powder. Asian: 2 tablespoons honey, 2 tablespoons teriyaki sauce, 2 teaspoons ground ginger. Sprinkle wings with 1 tablespoon sesame seeds. Zesty Honey-Dijon: Substitute the following blend instead of the **RedHot** butter mixture: ¼ cup each **Frank's® RedHot®** Sauce, **French's®** Honey Dijon Mustard and honey.

Prep Time: *5 minutes*
Cook Time: *12 minutes*

Herbed Potato Chips

Nonstick olive oil cooking spray
2 medium red potatoes (about ½ pound), unpeeled
1 tablespoon olive oil
2 tablespoons minced fresh dill, thyme or rosemary *or* 2 teaspoons dried dill weed, thyme or rosemary leaves, crushed
¼ teaspoon garlic salt
⅛ teaspoon black pepper
1¼ cups sour cream

1. Preheat oven to 450°F. Spray large baking sheets with cooking spray; set aside.

2. Cut potatoes crosswise into very thin slices, about ¹⁄₁₆ inch thick. Pat dry with paper towels. Arrange potato slices in single layer on prepared baking sheets; coat potatoes with cooking spray.

3. Bake 10 minutes; turn slices over. Brush with oil. Combine dill, garlic salt and pepper in small bowl; sprinkle evenly onto potato slices. Continue baking 5 to 10 minutes or until potatoes are golden brown. Cool on baking sheets. Serve with sour cream.

Makes 6 servings

Wings & Things

Angel Wings

Slow Cooker Directions

1. Combine soup, water, brown sugar, vinegar and shallots in slow cooker; mix well.

2. Add chicken wings; stir to coat with sauce.

3. Cover; cook on LOW 5 to 6 hours or until cooked through and glazed with sauce.
Makes 2 servings

1 can (10¾ ounces) condensed tomato soup, undiluted
¾ cup water
¼ cup packed light brown sugar
2½ tablespoons balsamic vinegar
2 tablespoons chopped shallots
10 chicken wings

3 to 4 pounds lean pork baby back ribs or spareribs

⅓ cup hoisin sauce

4 tablespoons soy sauce, divided

3 tablespoons dry sherry

3 cloves garlic, minced

2 tablespoons honey

1 tablespoon dark sesame oil

Barbecued Ribs

1. Place ribs in large resealable plastic food storage bag. Combine hoisin sauce, 3 tablespoons soy sauce, sherry and garlic in cup; pour over ribs. Seal bag; turn to coat. Marinate in refrigerator at least 4 hours or up to 24 hours.

2. Preheat oven to 375°F. Drain ribs; reserve marinade. Place ribs on rack in shallow, foil-lined roasting pan. Bake 30 minutes. Turn; brush ribs with half of reserved marinade. Bake 15 minutes. Turn ribs over; brush with remaining marinade. Bake 15 minutes.

3. Combine remaining 1 tablespoon soy sauce, honey and sesame oil in small bowl; brush over ribs. Bake 5 to 10 minutes or until ribs are browned and crisp.* Cut into serving-size pieces. *Makes 8 servings*

Ribs may be made ahead to this point. Cover and refrigerate up to 3 days. To reheat, wrap ribs in foil; cook in preheated 350°F oven 40 minutes or until heated through. Cut into serving-size pieces.

Jerk Wings with Ranch Dipping Sauce

1. Preheat oven to 450°F. For Ranch Dipping Sauce, combine mayonnaise, sour cream, ½ teaspoon salt, ¼ teaspoon garlic powder, ¼ teaspoon black pepper and onion powder in small bowl.

2. Combine orange juice, sugar, thyme, paprika, nutmeg, red pepper and remaining 1 teaspoon salt, 1 teaspoon garlic powder and ¼ teaspoon black pepper in small bowl.

3. Cut tips from wings; discard. Place wings in large bowl. Drizzle with orange juice mixture; toss to coat. Transfer chicken to greased broiler pan. Bake 25 to 30 minutes or until juices run clear and skin is crisp. Serve with Ranch Dipping Sauce.   *Makes 6 to 7 servings*

Serving Suggestion: Serve with celery sticks.

½ cup mayonnaise
½ cup sour cream or plain yogurt
1½ teaspoons salt, divided
1¼ teaspoons garlic powder, divided
½ teaspoon black pepper, divided
¼ teaspoon onion powder
2 tablespoons orange juice
1 teaspoon sugar
1 teaspoon dried thyme leaves
1 teaspoon paprika
¼ teaspoon *each* ground nutmeg and ground red pepper
2½ pounds chicken wings (about 10 wings)

Can't Get Enough Chicken Wings

18 chicken wings (about
   3 pounds)
 1 envelope LIPTON®
   RECIPE SECRETS®
   Savory Herb with
   Garlic Soup Mix
½ cup water
 2 to 3 tablespoons hot
   pepper sauce*
   (optional)
 2 tablespoons margarine or
   butter

1. Cut tips off chicken wings (save tips for soup). Cut chicken wings in half at joint. Deep fry, bake or broil until golden brown and crunchy.

2. Meanwhile, in small saucepan, combine soup mix, water and hot pepper sauce. Cook over low heat, stirring occasionally, 2 minutes or until thickened. Remove from heat and stir in margarine.

3. In large bowl, toss cooked chicken wings with hot soup mixture until evenly coated. Serve, if desired, over greens with cut-up celery.

Makes 36 appetizers

Use more or less hot pepper sauce as desired.

Baked Garlic Bundles

1. Preheat oven to 350°F. Remove phyllo from package; unroll and place on large sheet of waxed paper. Using scissors, cut phyllo crosswise into 2-inch-wide strips. Cover with large sheet of waxed paper and damp kitchen towel. (Phyllo dries out quickly if not covered.)

2. Lay 1 phyllo strip on flat surface; brush immediately with melted butter. Place 1 clove garlic at end of strip. Sprinkle about 1 teaspoon walnuts over length of strip. Roll up garlic clove and walnuts in strip, tucking in side edges. Brush bundle with melted butter; roll in bread crumbs to coat. Repeat with remaining phyllo strips, garlic cloves, walnuts, butter and bread crumbs.

3. Place bundles on rack in shallow roasting pan. Bake 20 minutes or until crispy.

Makes 24 to 27 appetizers

½ (16-ounce) package frozen phyllo dough, thawed to room temperature
¾ cup butter, melted
3 large heads garlic, separated into cloves and peeled
½ cup finely chopped walnuts
1 cup Italian-style bread crumbs

Hot & Spicy Buffalo Chicken Wings

1 can (15 ounces) DEL MONTE® Original Sloppy Joe Sauce

¼ cup thick and chunky salsa, medium

1 tablespoon red wine vinegar or cider vinegar

20 chicken wings (about 4 pounds)

1. Preheat oven to 400°F. Combine sloppy joe sauce, salsa and vinegar in small bowl. Remove ¼ cup sauce mixture to serve with cooked chicken wings; cover and refrigerate. Set aside remaining sauce mixture.

2. Arrange wings in single layer in large, shallow baking pan; brush wings with remaining sauce mixture.

3. Bake chicken, uncovered, on middle rack in oven 35 minutes or until chicken is no longer pink in center, turning and brushing with remaining sauce mixture after 15 minutes. Serve with reserved ¼ cup sauce. Garnish, if desired.

Makes 4 servings

Prep Time: *5 minutes*
Cook Time: *35 minutes*

Savory Corn Cakes

1. Combine flour, baking powder and salt in large bowl with wire whisk. Stir in corn, cheese, milk, egg whites, egg, green onions, garlic and chili powder until well blended.

2. Spray large nonstick skillet with nonstick cooking spray; heat over medium-high heat.

3. Drop batter by ¼ cupfuls into skillet. Cook 3 minutes per side or until golden brown. Serve with prepared salsa, if desired.

Makes 12 cakes

2 cups all-purpose flour
1 teaspoon baking powder
½ teaspoon salt
2 cups frozen corn, thawed
1 cup (4 ounces) shredded smoked Cheddar cheese
1 cup fat-free (skim) milk
2 egg whites, beaten
1 whole egg, beaten
4 green onions, finely chopped
2 cloves garlic, minced
1 tablespoon chili powder
Prepared salsa (optional)

Mariachi Chicken

1¼ cups crushed tortilla
   chips
1 package (1 ounce)
   LAWRY'S® Taco Spices
   & Seasonings
1 pound boneless chicken
   breasts *or* 2 dozen
   chicken drummettes
Salsa and sour cream
   (optional)

In large resealable plastic bag, combine chips and Taco Spices & Seasonings.

Dampen chicken with water; shake off excess. Place a few pieces at a time in bag; seal and shake to coat with chips. Arrange in greased shallow baking pan.

Bake, uncovered, in preheated 350°F oven for 40 to 45 minutes or until chicken is thoroughly cooked. Serve with salsa and sour cream, if desired.

Makes 24 appetizers

Prep Time: *5 to 10 minutes*
Cook Time: *40 to 45 minutes*

Hawaiian Ribs

1. Combine crushed pineapple with juice, apricot jam, mustard, vinegar, ginger and garlic in blender or food processor. Cover and process until very smooth.

2. Place ribs on oiled grid. Grill ribs over medium heat 40 minutes or until ribs are no longer pink near bone. Brush ribs with portion of pineapple sauce mixture during last 10 minutes of cooking.

3. Cut into individual ribs to serve. Serve remaining sauce for dipping.

Makes 8 servings (1½ cups sauce)

Note: Try mixing 2 tablespoons *French's®* Mustard, any flavor, with ¾ cup peach-apricot sweet 'n' sour sauce to create a delicious luau fruit dip. Serve with assorted cut-up fresh fruit.

Prep Time: *10 minutes*
Cook Time: *40 minutes*

1 can (8 ounces) crushed
    pineapple in juice,
    undrained
⅓ cup apricot jam
3 tablespoons *French's®*
    Classic Yellow®
    Mustard
1 tablespoon red wine
    vinegar
2 teaspoons grated peeled
    fresh ginger
1 clove garlic, minced
3 to 4 pounds pork baby
    back ribs

Buffalo Chicken Tenders

3 tablespoons Louisiana-
style hot sauce
½ teaspoon paprika
¼ teaspoon ground red
pepper
1 pound chicken tenders
½ cup blue cheese dressing
¼ cup sour cream
2 tablespoons crumbled
blue cheese
1 medium red bell pepper,
cut lengthwise into
½-inch-thick slices

1. Preheat oven to 375°F. Combine hot sauce, paprika and ground red pepper in small bowl; brush onto all surfaces of chicken. Place chicken in greased 11×7-inch baking dish. Cover; marinate in refrigerator 30 minutes.

2. Bake, uncovered, about 15 minutes or until chicken is no longer pink in center.

3. Combine blue cheese dressing, sour cream and blue cheese in small serving bowl. Garnish as desired. Serve with chicken and bell pepper for dipping.

Makes 10 servings

Wings & Things

One Potato, Two Potato

1. Preheat oven to 425°F. Spray baking sheet with cooking spray; set aside.

2. Spray cut sides of potatoes generously with cooking spray; sprinkle lightly with salt, if desired.

3. Combine bread crumbs, Parmesan cheese and desired herb in shallow dish. Add potatoes; toss lightly until potatoes are generously coated with crumb mixture. Place on prepared baking sheet. Bake potatoes until browned and tender, about 20 minutes. Serve warm with mustard for dipping, if desired.

Makes 4 servings

Potato Sweets: Omit bread crumbs, Parmesan cheese, oregano and mustard. Substitute sweet potatoes for baking potatoes. Cut and spray potatoes as directed; coat generously with desired amount of cinnamon-sugar. Bake as directed. Serve warm with peach or pineapple preserves or honey mustard for dipping. Makes 4 servings.

Nonstick cooking spray
2 medium baking potatoes,
    cut lengthwise into
    4 wedges
Salt (optional)
½ cup unseasoned dry
    bread crumbs
2 tablespoons grated
    Parmesan cheese
1½ teaspoons dried oregano
    leaves, dill weed,
    Italian herbs or paprika
Spicy brown or honey
    mustard, ketchup or
    reduced-fat sour cream
    (optional)

Dips & Spreads

Nutty Bacon Cheeseball

1 package (8 ounces)
   cream cheese, softened
½ cup milk
2 cups (8 ounces) *each*
   shredded sharp
   Cheddar and shredded
   Monterey Jack cheeses
¼ cup (1 ounce) crumbled
   blue cheese
10 slices bacon, crisp-
   cooked, crumbled
   and divided
¾ cup finely chopped
   pecans, divided
¼ cup finely minced green
   onions (white parts
   only)
1 jar (2 ounces) diced
   pimiento, drained
   Salt and black pepper
¼ cup minced fresh parsley
1 tablespoon poppy seeds

1. Beat cream cheese and milk in large bowl with electric mixer at low speed until blended. Add cheeses. Beat at medium speed until well mixed. Add half of bacon, half of pecans and green onions and pimiento. Beat at medium speed until well mixed. Add salt and pepper to taste.

2. Transfer half of cheese mixture to large piece of plastic wrap. Shape into ball; wrap tightly. Repeat with remaining mixture. Refrigerate at least 2 hours or until chilled.

3. Combine remaining bacon and pecans with parsley and poppy seeds in pie plate or large dinner plate. Remove plastic wrap from chilled cheese balls. Roll in bacon mixture until well coated. Wrap each ball tightly in plastic wrap; refrigerate until ready to serve, up to 24 hours. *Makes about 24 servings*

Party Cheese Spread

1 cup ricotta cheese
6 ounces cream cheese,
    softened
1 medium onion, chopped
2 tablespoons grated
    Parmesan cheese
1 tablespoon drained
    capers
2 anchovy fillets, mashed
    or 2 teaspoons
    anchovy paste
1 teaspoon dry mustard
1 teaspoon paprika
½ teaspoon hot pepper
    sauce
Red cabbage or bell
    pepper, for serving
Crackers and raw
    vegetables

1. Beat ricotta cheese and cream cheese in large bowl with electric mixer at medium speed until well blended. Stir in onion, Parmesan cheese, capers, anchovies, mustard, paprika and hot pepper sauce; mix well. Cover; refrigerate at least 1 day or up to 1 week to allow flavors to blend.

2. Just before serving, remove and discard any damaged outer leaves from cabbage. Slice small piece from bottom, so cabbage will sit flat. Cut out and remove inside portion of cabbage, leaving 1-inch-thick shell. (Be careful not to cut through bottom of cabbage.)

3. Spoon cheese spread into hollowed-out cabbage. Garnish, if desired. Serve with crackers and raw vegetables. *Makes about 2 cups*

Dips & Spreads

Chutney Cheese Spread

1. Place cream cheese and Cheddar cheese in food processor or blender. Cover; process until smooth.

2. Stir in chutney, green onions, raisins, garlic, curry powder, coriander and ginger, to taste. Cover; refrigerate 2 to 3 hours.

3. Top spread with peanuts. Serve with additional green onions and melba toast, if desired.

Makes about 20 servings

Tip: This spread can also be garnished with one tablespoon toasted coconut, lending a slightly sweeter flavor.

- **2 packages (8 ounces each) fat-free cream cheese, softened**
- **1 cup (4 ounces) shredded reduced-fat Cheddar cheese**
- **½ cup mango chutney**
- **¼ cup thinly sliced green onions with tops**
- **3 tablespoons dark raisins, chopped**
- **2 cloves garlic, minced**
- **1 to 1½ teaspoons curry powder**
- **¾ teaspoon ground coriander**
- **½ to ¾ teaspoon ground ginger**
- **1 tablespoon chopped dry-roasted peanuts**

Tomato-Pesto Stuffed Brie

1 cup boiling water
1 package (3 ounces) unsalted sun-dried tomatoes (about 2 cups)
4 tablespoons *Frank's® RedHot®* Original Cayenne Pepper Sauce
2 green onions, chopped
2 (5-inch) whole Brie, about 13 ounces each, well chilled
1 jar (1¾ ounces) pine nuts, toasted*
3 tablespoons butter, softened
¾ cup chopped fresh parsley

1. Pour boiling water over tomatoes in medium bowl. Let stand 4 minutes or until just softened; drain well and pat dry with paper towels. Place tomatoes, *Frank's RedHot* Sauce and onions in food processor; process until smooth paste forms.

2. Using large sharp knife, split each Brie round in half horizontally. Spread tomato mixture over cut sides of bottom halves. Sprinkle evenly with pine nuts. Cover bottom halves with top halves, cut side down. Press gently.

3. Spread butter on edges of rounds; roll in chopped parsley. Refrigerate about 1 hour. Cut into wedges; serve with crackers or French bread.

Makes 12 servings

To toast pine nuts, bake at 350°F 5 minutes or until golden.

Note: Filled Brie may be served warm. (Do not coat with butter and parsley.) Place in baking dish; bake at 325°F 5 to 10 minutes or until slightly softened.

Prep Time: *30 minutes*
Chill Time: *1 hour*

Roasted Red Pepper Spread

Blot dry red peppers. In a food processor fitted with a metal blade, combine peppers, cream cheese and salad dressing & seasoning mix; process until smooth. Spread on baguette slices and garnish with olives, if desired.

Makes 2 cups

1 cup roasted red peppers, rinsed and drained
1 package (8 ounces) cream cheese, softened
1 packet (1 ounce) HIDDEN VALLEY® The Original Ranch® Salad Dressing & Seasoning Mix
Baguette slices and sliced ripe olives (optional)

Dips & Spreads

Nutty Broccoli Spread

1 box (10 ounces) BIRDS
    EYE® frozen Chopped
    Broccoli
4 ounces cream cheese
¼ cup grated Parmesan
    cheese
1 teaspoon dried basil
¼ cup walnuts
1 loaf frozen garlic bread

• Cook broccoli according to package directions; drain well.

• Place broccoli, cream cheese, Parmesan cheese and basil in food processor or blender; process until ingredients are mixed. (Do not overmix.) Add walnuts; process 3 to 5 seconds.

• Split garlic bread lengthwise. Spread broccoli mixture evenly over bread. Bake in preheated 350° oven for 10 to 15 minutes or until bread is toasted and broccoli mixture is heated through. Cut bread into slices; serve hot.

Makes about 2 cups spread

Prep Time: *10 minutes*
Cook Time: *10 to 15 minutes*

Dips & Spreads

Roasted Garlic Spread
with Three Cheeses

1. Preheat oven to 400°F. Cut tops off garlic heads to expose tops of cloves. Place garlic in small baking pan; bake 45 minutes or until very tender. Remove from pan; cool completely. Squeeze garlic into small bowl; mash with fork.

2. Beat cream cheese and goat cheese in small bowl until smooth; stir in blue cheese, garlic and thyme. Cover; refrigerate 3 hours or overnight.

3. Spoon dip into serving bowl; serve with cucumbers, radishes, carrots and yellow bell peppers. Garnish with fresh thyme and red bell pepper, if desired.

Makes 21 servings

2 medium heads garlic
2 packages (8 ounces each) fat-free cream cheese, softened
1 package (3½ ounces) goat cheese
2 tablespoons (1 ounce) crumbled blue cheese
1 teaspoon dried thyme leaves
Assorted sliced fresh vegetables
Fresh thyme and red bell pepper, for garnish (optional)

Honey-Nut Glazed Brie

8 ounces Brie cheese
  (wedge or round)
¼ cup I CAN'T BELIEVE
  IT'S NOT BUTTER!®
  Spread
1 cup coarsely chopped
  walnuts
¼ teaspoon ground
  cinnamon (optional)
⅛ teaspoon ground nutmeg
  (optional)
2 tablespoons honey
2 large green and/or red
  apples, cored and
  thinly sliced

Arrange cheese* on serving platter; set aside.

In 10-inch nonstick skillet, melt I Can't Believe It's Not Butter!® Spread over medium-high heat and stir in walnuts until coated.

Stir in cinnamon and nutmeg until blended. Stir in honey and cook, stirring constantly, 2 minutes or until mixture is bubbling. Immediately pour over cheese. Serve hot with apples.   *Makes 8 servings*

If desired, on microwave-safe plate, arrange cheese and top with cooked nut mixture. Microwave at HIGH (Full Power) 1 minute or until cheese is warm. OR, in 1-quart shallow casserole, arrange cheese and top with cooked nut mixture. Bake at 350°F. for 10 minutes or until Brie just begins to melt. Serve as above.

Summer Fruits with Peanut Butter-Honey Dip

1. Place peanut butter in small bowl; gradually stir in milk and honey until blended.

2. Stir in apple juice and cinnamon until mixture is smooth.

3. Serve dip with prepared fruits.

Makes 4 servings (about ½ cup dip)

⅓ cup smooth or chunky peanut butter
2 tablespoons milk
2 tablespoons honey
1 tablespoon apple juice or water
⅛ teaspoon ground cinnamon
2 cups melon balls, including cantaloupe and honeydew
1 peach or nectarine, pitted and cut into 8 wedges
1 banana, peeled and thickly sliced

Roasted Eggplant Spread

1 large eggplant
1 can (14½ ounces) diced
  tomatoes, drained
½ cup finely chopped green
  onions
½ cup chopped fresh
  parsley
2 tablespoons red wine
  vinegar
1 tablespoon olive oil
3 cloves garlic, finely
  chopped
½ teaspoon salt
½ teaspoon dried oregano
  leaves
2 (8-inch) pita bread
  rounds
  Fresh lemon and lime
  slices, for garnish
  (optional)

1. Preheat oven to 375°F. Place eggplant on baking sheet. Bake 1 hour or until tender, turning occasionally. Remove eggplant from oven. Let stand 10 minutes or until cool enough to handle.

2. Cut eggplant in half lengthwise; remove pulp. Discard stem and skin. Place pulp in medium bowl; mash with fork until smooth. Add tomatoes, onions, parsley, vinegar, oil, garlic, salt and oregano; blend well. Cover eggplant mixture; refrigerate 2 hours.

3. Preheat broiler. Split pita bread rounds horizontally in half to form 4 rounds. Stack pita rounds; cut into sixths to form 24 wedges. Place wedges on baking sheet. Broil 4 inches from heat 3 minutes or until crisp. Serve eggplant spread with warm pita bread wedges. Garnish with lemon and lime slices, if desired.

Makes 4 servings

Shrimp Spread

1. Place reserved shrimp shells, water, onion powder and garlic salt in medium saucepan. Bring to a simmer over medium heat; simmer 5 minutes. Remove shells; discard. Add shrimp; simmer 1 minute or until shrimp turn pink and opaque. Remove shrimp and place on cutting board; let cool. Continue cooking shrimp liquid to reduce until just barely covering bottom of pan.

2. Blend cream cheese, butter, mayonnaise, cocktail sauce and lemon juice in large bowl until smooth. Stir in 1 tablespoon reduced cooking liquid. Discard remaining liquid.

3. Chop shrimp finely. Fold shrimp and parsley into cream cheese mixture. Pack shrimp spread into decorative serving crock or mold lined with plastic wrap. Cover; refrigerate overnight. Serve shrimp spread in decorative crock, or invert mold onto serving platter and remove plastic wrap. Serve with assorted crackers or raw vegetables. Garnish as desired.

Makes 2½ to 3 cups

½ **pound raw medium shrimp, peeled and deveined, shells reserved**
1 **cup water**
½ **teaspoon onion powder**
½ **teaspoon garlic salt**
1 **package (8 ounces) cream cheese, softened**
4 **tablespoons butter, softened**
2 **tablespoons mayonnaise**
2 **tablespoons cocktail sauce**
1 **tablespoon lemon juice**
1 **tablespoon chopped fresh parsley**
Assorted crackers or raw vegetables

Nutty Carrot Spread

¼ cup finely chopped pecans

6 ounces cream cheese, softened

2 tablespoons frozen orange juice concentrate, thawed

¼ teaspoon ground cinnamon

1 cup shredded carrot

¼ cup raisins

36 party pumpernickel bread slices, toasted, or melba toast rounds

1. Preheat oven to 350°F. Place pecans in shallow baking pan. Bake 10 minutes or until lightly toasted, stirring occasionally.

2. Meanwhile, combine cream cheese, orange juice concentrate and cinnamon in small bowl; stir until well blended. Stir in carrot, pecans and raisins.

3. Serve carrot spread with bread or crackers. Garnish, if desired.

Makes 18 servings

Baked Brie

1. Preheat oven to 350°F. Place cheese in shallow oven-safe serving dish. Top with pecans and corn syrup.

2. Bake 8 to 10 minutes or until cheese is almost melted.

3. Serve warm with plain crackers or melba toast.

Makes 8 servings

Prep Time: *3 minutes*
Cook Time: *10 minutes*

½ **pound Brie cheese, rind removed**
¼ **cup chopped pecans**
¼ **cup KARO® Dark Corn Syrup**

Dips & Spreads

Roasted Garlic Hummus

2 tablespoons Roasted
    Garlic (recipe follows)
1 can (15 ounces) chick-
    peas (garbanzo beans),
    rinsed and drained
¼ cup fresh parsley, stems
    removed
2 tablespoons lemon juice
2 tablespoons water
½ teaspoon curry powder
⅛ teaspoon dark sesame oil
    Dash hot pepper sauce
    Pita bread and fresh
    vegetables

1 Prepare Roasted Garlic.

2. Place chick-peas, parsley, 2 tablespoons Roasted Garlic, lemon juice, water, curry powder, sesame oil and hot pepper sauce in food processor or blender. Cover; process until smooth, scraping down side of bowl once.

3. Serve hummus with pita bread triangles and fresh vegetables.

Makes 6 servings

Roasted Garlic: Cut off top third of 1 large garlic head (not the root end) to expose cloves; discard top. Place head of garlic, trimmed end up, on 10-inch square of foil. Rub garlic generously with olive oil and sprinkle with salt. Gather foil ends together and close tightly. Roast in preheated 350°F oven 45 minutes or until cloves are golden and soft. When cool enough to handle, squeeze roasted garlic cloves from skins; discard skins.

Seafood Spread

1. Beat cream cheese in medium bowl with electric mixer at medium speed until smooth. Add whitefish, green onion, dill, lemon juice and pepper; mix until well blended.

2. Refrigerate until ready to serve.

3. Serve with rye bread slices and garnish with lime wedges, if desired.

Makes 12 servings (1½ cups)

1 package (8 ounces) cream cheese, softened
½ pound smoked whitefish, skinned, boned and flaked
2 tablespoons minced green onion
1 tablespoon plus 1 teaspoon chopped fresh dill
1 teaspoon lemon juice
¼ teaspoon black pepper
Rye bread halves
Lime wedges, for garnish (optional)

Best of the Wurst Spread

1 tablespoon butter or
   margarine
½ cup finely chopped onion
1 package (16 ounces)
   liverwurst
¼ cup mayonnaise or salad
   dressing
¼ cup finely chopped dill
   pickle
1 tablespoon drained
   capers
2 teaspoons horseradish
   mustard or spicy
   brown mustard
2 teaspoons dried dill weed
¼ small dill pickle, cut into
   strips
   Crackers or cocktail rye
   bread

1. Heat butter in small saucepan over medium heat until melted. Add onion; cook and stir 5 minutes or until tender. Set aside.

2. Mash liverwurst with fork in medium bowl; beat in onion, mayonnaise, chopped dill pickle, capers, mustard and dill weed.

3. Form liverwurst mixture into football shape on serving plate; decorate with dill pickle strips to look like football laces. Serve with crackers.

Makes 12 (3-tablespoon) servings

Serving Suggestion: For added flavor, serve this spread with mustard toast instead of rye bread. To prepare mustard toast, lightly spread horseradish mustard or spicy brown mustard onto cocktail rye bread slices. Broil 4 inches from heat until lightly browned.

Baked Apricot Brie

1. Preheat oven to 400°F. Place cheese in small baking pan. Spread top of cheese with preserves; sprinkle with almonds.

2. Bake about 10 to 12 minutes or until cheese begins to melt and lose its shape.

3. Serve hot with crackers. Refrigerate leftovers; reheat before serving.

Makes 6 servings

Note: Brie is a soft-ripened, unpressed cheese made from cow's milk. It has a distinctive round shape, edible white rind and creamy yellow interior. Avoid Brie that has a chalky center (it is underripe) or a strong ammonia odor (it is overripe). The cheese should give slightly to pressure and have an evenly colored, barely moist rind.

1 round (8 ounces) Brie cheese
¹⁄₃ cup apricot preserves
2 tablespoons sliced almonds
Cracked pepper or other assorted crackers

Mexican Fiesta

Miniature Quesadillas

½ teaspoon chili powder
½ teaspoon ground cumin
¼ teaspoon salt
½ teaspoon dried oregano
   leaves
1 cup shredded Cheddar
   cheese
½ cup (about 2 ounces)
   shredded Monterey
   Jack cheese
8 teaspoons CRISCO® Oil,
   divided
8 (6-inch) flour tortillas
   Fresh salsa (optional)

Combine chili powder, cumin, salt and oregano in large resealable plastic bag. Add Cheddar and Monterey Jack cheeses. Shake to coat cheese.

Heat 2 teaspoons CRISCO® Oil in each of 2 heavy large skillets over medium-high heat. Add 1 tortilla to each skillet. Top each with ¼ cheese mixture. Top each with 1 tortilla. Cook until bottoms are golden brown, about 3 minutes. Turn quesadillas over. Cook until bottoms are golden brown and cheese melts, about 3 minutes.

Transfer to cutting board. Cut each quesadilla into 4 wedges. Transfer to platter. Repeat with remaining CRISCO® Oil, tortillas and cheese mixture. Top with salsa, if desired. Serve hot. *Makes 4 servings*

Taco Chicken Nachos

2 boneless skinless chicken breasts (about 8 ounces)
1 tablespoon plus 1½ teaspoons taco seasoning mix
1 teaspoon olive oil
¾ cup sour cream
1 can (4 ounces) chopped mild green chilies, drained
¼ cup minced red onion
1 bag (8 ounces) tortilla chips
1 cup (4 ounces) shredded Cheddar or Monterey Jack cheese
½ cup chopped fresh tomato
¼ cup pitted ripe olive slices (optional)
2 tablespoons chopped fresh cilantro (optional)

1. Bring 2 cups water to a boil in small saucepan. Add chicken. Reduce heat to low; cover. Simmer 10 minutes or until chicken is no longer pink in center. Remove from saucepan; cool. Chop chicken.

2. Combine taco seasoning mix and oil in small bowl; mix until smooth paste forms. Stir in sour cream. Add chicken, green chilies and onion; mix lightly.

3. Preheat broiler. Arrange tortilla chips on small ovenproof plates or large platter. Cover chips with chicken mixture and cheese. Broil 4 inches from heat 2 to 3 minutes or until chicken mixture is hot and cheese is melted. Sprinkle evenly with tomato, olives and cilantro, if desired. Serve hot.

Makes 12 servings

Nachos con Queso y Cerveza

1. Preheat oven to 350°F. Place chips in 13×9-inch baking pan; set aside.

2. Spray large nonstick skillet with cooking spray. Heat over medium heat until hot. Add onion, peppers, garlic, chili powder and cumin. Cook 5 minutes or until vegetables are tender, stirring occasionally. Stir in chicken, tomatoes and pilsner. Simmer until liquid is absorbed.

3. Spoon chicken-tomato mixture over chips; top with cheese and olives. Bake 5 minutes or until cheese melts. Serve immediately.   *Makes 4 servings*

*Jalapeño peppers can sting and irritate the skin. Wear rubber gloves when handling peppers and do not touch eyes. Wash hands after handling.

4 ounces tortilla chips
   Nonstick cooking spray
¾ cup chopped red onion
2 jalapeño peppers,*
   seeded and chopped
3 cloves garlic, finely
   chopped
2 teaspoons chili powder
½ teaspoon ground cumin
2 boneless skinless
   chicken breasts (about
   8 ounces), cooked and
   chopped
1 can (14½ ounces)
   Mexican-style diced
   tomatoes, drained
⅓ cup pilsner lager
1 cup (4 ounces) shredded
   Monterey Jack cheese
2 tablespoons black olives,
   chopped

Mexican Fiesta

Fast Guacamole and "Chips"

2 ripe avocados
½ cup restaurant-style chunky salsa
¼ teaspoon hot pepper sauce (optional)
½ seedless cucumber, sliced into ⅛-inch-thick rounds

1. Cut avocados in half; remove and discard pits. Scoop flesh into medium bowl; mash with fork.

2. Add salsa and hot pepper sauce, if desired; mix well.

3. Transfer guacamole to serving bowl; surround with cucumber "chips."

Makes 8 servings

New-Age Quesadillas

Place 4 tortillas on sheet of waxed paper. Sprinkle ¼ cup cheese over each tortilla. Arrange roasted peppers and French Fried Onions evenly over cheese. Sprinkle remaining cheese over onion layer. Top each layered tortilla with another tortilla, pressing down firmly.

Heat nonstick skillet over medium heat; spray with nonstick cooking spray. Using large spatula, place 1 quesadilla in skillet. Cook, pressing down with spatula, 2 to 3 minutes per side or until cheese melts and tortillas brown slightly. Repeat with remaining quesadillas.

To serve, cut each quesadilla into fourths. Serve with salsa, if desired.

Makes 4 to 6 appetizer servings

Prep Time: 20 minutes
Cook Time: 10 minutes

**8 whole wheat tortillas
(7 inches)
2 cups (8 ounces) shredded
Monterey Jack cheese
with jalapeño peppers,
divided
1 jar (7 ounces) roasted red
peppers, drained and
thinly sliced
1⅓ cups *French's*® French
Fried Onions
Salsa (optional)**

Fiesta Chicken Nachos

1 tablespoon olive oil
1 pound boneless, skinless
   chicken breasts
1 jar (1 pound) RAGÚ®
   Cheese Creations!®
   Double Cheddar Sauce
1 bag (9 ounces) tortilla
   chips
2 green and/or red bell
   peppers, diced
1 small onion, chopped
1 large tomato, diced

In 12-inch skillet, heat olive oil over medium-high heat and cook chicken, stirring occasionally, 8 minutes or until thoroughly cooked. Remove from skillet; cut into strips.

In same skillet, combine chicken and Ragú Cheese Creations! Double Cheddar Sauce; heat through.

On serving platter, arrange layer of tortilla chips, then ½ of the sauce mixture, bell peppers, onion and tomato; repeat, ending with tomato. Garnish, if desired, with chopped fresh cilantro and shredded lettuce.   *Makes 4 servings*

Tip: For a spicier dish, add chopped jalapeño peppers or hot pepper sauce.

Bite Size Tacos

1. Cook beef in nonstick skillet over medium-high heat 5 minutes or until browned; drain. Stir In taco seasoning mix, ¾ cup water, 1 cup French Fried Onions and cilantro. Simmer 5 minutes or until flavors are blended, stirring often.

2. Preheat oven to 350°F. Arrange tortilla chips on foil-lined baking sheet. Top with beef mixture, sour cream, remaining onions and cheese.

3. Bake 5 minutes or until cheese is melted and onions are golden.

Makes 8 appetizer servings

Prep Time: *5 minutes*
Cook Time: *15 minutes*

1 pound ground beef
1 package (1.25 ounces) taco seasoning mix
2 cups *French's®* French Fried Onions
¼ cup chopped fresh cilantro
32 bite-size round tortilla chips
¾ cup sour cream
1 cup shredded Cheddar cheese

Cheesy Pepper & Onion Quesadillas

⅓ cup margarine

3¾ cups frozen vegetable stir-fry blend (onions and red, yellow and green bell peppers)

¾ teaspoon chili powder

1 package (8 ounces) fat-free cream cheese, softened

1 package (8 ounces) shredded fat-free Cheddar cheese

10 (6-inch) flour tortillas

Salsa (optional)

1. Preheat oven to 425°F.

2. Heat margarine in large nonstick skillet over medium heat until melted. Add stir-fry blend and chili powder; cook and stir until tender. Drain, reserving margarine.

3. Beat cream cheese with electric mixer at medium speed until smooth. Add Cheddar cheese, mixing until blended. Spread 2 tablespoons cheese mixture onto each tortilla; top with pepper mixture. Fold tortillas in half; place on baking sheet. Brush with reserved margarine. Bake 10 minutes. Cut each tortilla in half. Serve warm with salsa, if desired. *Makes 20 appetizers*

Nachos à la Ortega®

PREHEAT broiler.

SPREAD beans over bottom of large ovenproof platter or 15×10-inch jelly-roll pan. Arrange chips over beans. Top with cheese and jalapeños.

BROIL for 1 to 1½ minutes or until cheese is melted. Top with desired toppings.

Makes 4 to 6 servings

1 can (16 ounces) ORTEGA® Refried Beans, warmed
4 cups baked tortilla chips
1½ cups (6 ounces) shredded Monterey Jack cheese
2 tablespoons ORTEGA Pickled Jalapeños, sliced

Suggested Toppings
ORTEGA Salsa-Thick & Chunky, sour cream, guacamole, sliced ripe olives, chopped green onions, chopped fresh cilantro (optional)

Mexican Fiesta

2 (6-inch) corn tortillas
½ cup (2 ounces) shredded
   sharp Cheddar cheese
2 tablespoons sour cream
¼ cup canned black beans,
   rinsed and drained
¼ cup salsa
¼ cup sliced ripe olives

Mexican Flats

1. Place 1 tortilla on each of 2 microwavable plates. Sprinkle ¼ cup cheese over each tortilla.

2. Cover each plate with waxed paper; microwave at HIGH 20 to 30 seconds or until cheese melts.

3. Carefully remove waxed paper. Spread 1 tablespoon sour cream over each tortilla. Top with black beans. Lightly mash beans with fork. Top each flat with salsa and olives. Serve open-face or fold in half.   *Makes 2 servings*

Hearty Ham Quesadillas

Preheat oven to 500°F.

Combine Ham, cheese, onion, jalapeño peppers, cilantro, black pepper and salt in large bowl. Arrange ⅛ of ham mixture on each tortilla, covering ½ of tortilla. Fold each tortilla over to make half-moons.

Place tortillas in shallow baking pan. Bake until tortillas are crisp and golden, about 5 minutes. Cut into wedges; serve with salsa.   *Makes 8 servings*

1 pound **HILLSHIRE FARM®** Ham, chopped
1 cup reduced-fat shredded Monterey Jack cheese
¼ cup minced onion
1 to 2 jalapeño peppers, seeded and minced
4 tablespoons minced cilantro
½ teaspoon black pepper
¼ teaspoon salt
8 (10-inch) flour tortillas
Prepared tomato salsa

Tex-Mex Potato Skins

3 hot baked potatoes, split lengthwise

¾ cup (3 ounces) shredded Cheddar or pepper Jack cheese

1⅓ cups *French's®* French Fried Onions, divided

¼ cup chopped green chilies

¼ cup crumbled cooked bacon

Salsa and sour cream

1. Preheat oven to 350°F. Scoop out inside of potatoes, leaving ¼-inch shells. Reserve inside of potatoes for another use.

2. Arrange potato halves on baking sheet. Top with cheese, ⅔ *cup* French Fried Onions, chilies and bacon.

3. Bake 15 minutes or until heated through and cheese is melted. Cut each potato half crosswise into thirds. Serve topped with salsa, sour cream and remaining onions.   *Makes 18 appetizer servings*

Tip: To bake potatoes quickly, microwave at HIGH 10 to 12 minutes or until tender.

Variation: For added Cheddar flavor, substitute *French's®* **Cheddar French Fried Onions** for the original flavor.

Prep Time: *15 minutes*
Cook Time: *15 minutes*

Hearty Nachos

1. In 12-inch nonstick skillet, brown ground beef over medium-high heat; drain.

2. Stir in soup mix, black beans and salsa. Bring to a boil over high heat. Reduce heat to low and simmer 5 minutes or until heated through.

3. Arrange tortilla chips on serving platter. Spread beef mixture over chips; sprinkle with Cheddar cheese. Top, if desired, with sliced green onions, sliced pitted ripe olives, chopped tomato and chopped cilantro.   *Makes 8 servings*

Prep Time: *10 minutes*
Cook Time: *12 minutes*

1 pound ground beef
1 envelope LIPTON®
RECIPE SECRETS®
Onion Soup Mix
1 can (19 ounces) black beans, rinsed and drained
1 cup prepared salsa
1 package (8½ ounces) plain tortilla chips
1 cup shredded Cheddar cheese (about 4 ounces)

4 (10-inch) flour tortillas, divided

¼ cup plus 2 tablespoons pinto or black bean dip

1 can (9 ounces) tuna packed in water, drained and flaked

2 cups (8 ounces) shredded Cheddar cheese

1 can (14½ ounces) diced tomatoes, drained

½ cup thinly sliced green onions

1½ teaspoons butter or margarine, melted

Tuna Quesadilla Stack

1. Preheat oven to 400°F.

2. Place 1 tortilla on 12-inch pizza pan. Spread with 2 tablespoons bean dip, leaving ½-inch border. Top with one third each of tuna, cheese, tomatoes and green onions. Repeat layers twice, beginning with tortilla and ending with onions. Top with remaining tortilla, pressing gently. Brush with melted butter.

3. Bake 15 minutes or until cheese melts and top is lightly browned. Cool. Cut into 8 wedges. *Makes 4 servings*

Tip: For a special touch, serve with assorted toppings, such as guacamole, sour cream and salsa.

Tex-Mex Guacamole Platter

1. Cut avocados in half; remove pits. Scoop out flesh into food processor. Add lime juice, garlic, olive oil, salt and pepper. Cover; process until almost smooth.

2. Spread avocado mixture evenly onto large dinner plate or serving platter, leaving border around edge.

3. Top with cheese, tomatoes, olives, salsa and cilantro. Serve with tortilla chips.

Makes 6 to 8 servings

4 ripe avocados
¼ cup lime juice
3 large cloves garlic, crushed
2 tablespoons olive oil
½ teaspoon salt
¼ teaspoon black pepper
1 cup (4 ounces) shredded Colby-Jack cheese
1 cup seeded, diced plum tomatoes
⅓ cup sliced pitted ripe olives
⅓ cup prepared salsa
1 tablespoon minced fresh cilantro
Tortilla chips

California Quesadillas

1 small ripe avocado
2 packages (3 ounces each) cream cheese, softened
3 tablespoons *Frank's® RedHot®* Original Cayenne Pepper Sauce
¼ cup minced fresh cilantro leaves
16 (6-inch) flour tortillas (2 packages)
1 cup (4 ounces) shredded Cheddar or Monterey Jack cheese
½ cup finely chopped green onions
Sour cream (optional)

Halve avocado and remove pit. Scoop out flesh into food processor or bowl of electric mixer. Add cream cheese and *Frank's RedHot* Sauce. Cover and process or beat until smooth. Add cilantro; process or beat until well blended.

Spread rounded tablespoon avocado mixture onto each tortilla. Sprinkle half the tortillas with cheese and onions, dividing evenly. Top with remaining tortillas; press gently.

Place tortillas on oiled grid. Grill over medium coals 5 minutes or until cheese melts and tortillas are lightly browned, turning once. Cut into triangles. Serve with sour cream, if desired. Garnish as desired.   *Makes 8 appetizer servings*

Note: You may serve avocado mixture as a dip with tortilla chips.

Prep Time: *20 minutes*
Cook Time: *5 minutes*

Taco Dip

1. Combine cream cheese, sour cream, chili powder, cumin and ground red pepper in large bowl; mix until well blended. Stir in salsa.

2. Spread dip onto greens-lined serving platter. Top with Cheddar cheese, Monterey Jack cheese, tomatoes, green onions, ripe olives and green olives.

3. Serve with tortilla chips and blue corn chips.

Makes 10 servings

12 ounces cream cheese, softened
½ cup sour cream
2 teaspoons chili powder
1½ teaspoons ground cumin
⅛ teaspoon ground red pepper
½ cup salsa
Crisp salad greens
1 cup (4 ounces) shredded Cheddar cheese
1 cup (4 ounces) shredded Monterey Jack cheese
½ cup diced plum tomatoes
⅓ cup sliced green onions
¼ cup sliced pitted ripe olives
¼ cup sliced pimiento-stuffed green olives
Tortilla chips and blue corn chips

Grilled Quesadilla Snacks

1½ cups (6 ounces) shredded Monterey Jack cheese

½ red or yellow bell pepper, chopped

2 ounces sliced smoked ham, cut into thin strips

2 ounces sliced smoked turkey, cut into thin strips

¼ cup finely chopped green onions

⅓ cup *French's*® Classic Yellow® Mustard

2 teaspoons ground cumin

10 flour tortillas (6 inch)

1. Combine cheese, bell pepper, ham, turkey and onions in medium bowl. Combine mustard and cumin in small bowl; mix well.

2. Place 5 tortillas on sheet of waxed paper. Spread 1 rounded teaspoon mustard mixture over each tortilla. Sprinkle cheese mixture evenly over mustard mixture. Top with another tortilla, pressing down firmly to form quesadilla.

3. Place quesadillas on oiled grid. Grill over medium heat 2 minutes or until cheese is melted and heated through, turning once. Cut each quesadilla into quarters. Serve with salsa and cilantro, if desired.   *Makes 10 servings*

Prep Time: *30 minutes*
Cook Time: *2 minutes*

Nachos Olé

1. Preheat oven to 400°F. Combine cheeses in small bowl.

2. Cook and stir beans in small saucepan over medium heat until hot. Spread 1 teaspoon beans onto each tortilla chip. Arrange chips in single layer on 2 to 3 baking sheets. Sprinkle chips evenly with tomato and chilies; sprinkle with cheese mixture.

3. Bake 5 to 8 minutes or until cheese is bubbly and melted.

Makes 6 to 8 servings

Jalapeño peppers can sting and irritate the skin. Wear rubber gloves when handling peppers and do not touch eyes. Wash hands after handling.

1½ cups (6 ounces) shredded Monterey Jack cheese
1½ cups (6 ounces) shredded Cheddar cheese
1½ cups refried beans
72 packaged corn tortilla chips
1 large tomato, seeded and chopped
½ cup pickled jalapeño peppers,* thinly sliced

Cheesy Quesadillas

½ pound ground beef
1 medium onion, chopped
¼ teaspoon salt
1 can (4½ ounces) chopped green chilies, drained
1 jar (1 pound 10 ounces) RAGÚ® Robusto!™ Pasta Sauce
8 (6½-inch) flour tortillas
1 tablespoon olive oil
2 cups shredded Cheddar and/or mozzarella cheese (about 8 ounces)

1. Preheat oven to 400°F. In 12-inch skillet, brown ground beef with onion and salt over medium-high heat; drain. Stir in chilies and ½ cup Ragú Pasta Sauce; set aside.

2. Meanwhile, evenly brush one side of 4 tortillas with half of the olive oil. On cookie sheets, arrange tortillas, oil-side down. Evenly top with ½ of the cheese, beef filling, then remaining cheese. Top with remaining 4 tortillas, then brush tops with remaining oil.

3. Bake 10 minutes or until cheese is melted. To serve, cut each quesadilla into 4 wedges. Serve with remaining sauce, heated.   Makes 4 servings

Prep Time: *10 minutes*
Cook Time: *15 minutes*

SPAM™ Nachos

Heat oven to 425°F. Place chips on baking sheet. Sprinkle SPAM® over chips. In medium bowl, combine salsa and refried beans; pour over chips. Sprinkle with cheese. Bake 6 to 7 minutes or until cheese is melted. Serve immediately.

Makes 10 appetizer servings

1 (10½-ounce) bag
CHI-CHI'S™ Tortilla
Chips
1 (12-ounce) can SPAM®
Classic, cubed
1 (16-ounce) jar
CHI-CHI'S® Salsa
1 (16-ounce) can refried
beans
1 (8-ounce) package
shredded Mexican
pasteurized processed
cheese

Mexican Fiesta

Festive Holidays

Festive Taco Cups

1 tablespoon vegetable oil
½ cup chopped onion
½ pound ground turkey or
    ground beef
1 clove garlic, minced
½ teaspoon dried oregano
    leaves
½ teaspoon chili powder or
    taco seasoning
¼ teaspoon salt
1¼ cups shredded taco-
    flavored cheese or
    Mexican cheese blend,
    divided
1 can (11½ ounces)
    refrigerated corn
    breadstick dough
Chopped fresh tomato
    and sliced green onion,
    for garnish (optional)

1. Heat oil in large skillet over medium heat. Add onion; cook until tender. Add turkey; cook until turkey is no longer pink, stirring occasionally. Stir in garlic, oregano, chili powder and salt. Remove from heat; stir in ½ cup cheese. Set aside.

2. Preheat oven to 375°F. Lightly grease 36 miniature (1¾-inch) muffin pan cups. Remove dough from container; *do not unroll dough.* Separate dough into 8 pieces at perforations. Divide each piece into 3 pieces; roll or pat each piece into 3-inch circle. Press circles into prepared muffin pan cups.

3. Fill each cup with 1½ to 2 teaspoons turkey mixture. Bake 10 minutes. Sprinkle tops of taco cups with remaining ¾ cup cheese; bake 2 to 3 minutes more or until cheese is melted. Garnish with tomato and green onion, if desired.

Makes 36 taco cups

Cheese Pinecones

2 cups (8 ounces) shredded
    Swiss cheese
½ cup butter or margarine,
    softened
3 tablespoons milk
2 tablespoons dry sherry or
    milk
⅛ teaspoon ground red
    pepper
1 cup finely chopped
    blanched almonds
¾ cup slivered blanched
    almonds
¾ cup sliced almonds
½ cup whole almonds
    Fresh rosemary sprigs
    Assorted crackers

1. Beat cheese, butter, milk, sherry and red pepper in medium bowl until smooth; stir in chopped almonds.

2. Divide mixture into 3 equal portions; shape each into tapered oval to resemble pinecone. Insert slivered, sliced or whole almonds into each cone. Cover; refrigerate 2 to 3 hours or until firm.

3. Arrange Cheese Pinecones on wooden board or serving plate. Garnish tops with rosemary sprigs. Serve with assorted crackers.

Makes 12 to 16 servings

Festive Holidays

Festive Franks

1. Preheat oven to 350°F. Spray large baking sheet with nonstick cooking spray; set aside.

2. Unroll dough and separate into 8 triangles. Cut each triangle in half lengthwise to make 16 triangles. Lightly spread barbecue sauce over triangles. Sprinkle with cheese.

3. Cut each hot dog in half; trim off rounded ends. Place 1 hot dog half at large end of dough triangle. Roll up jelly-roll style from wide end. Place, point side down, on prepared baking sheet. Sprinkle with poppy seeds, if desired. Repeat with remaining hot dog halves and dough. Bake 13 minutes or until dough is golden brown. Cool 1 to 2 minutes on baking sheet. Serve with additional barbecue sauce for dipping, if desired. *Makes 16 servings*

1 can (8 ounces) crescent
   roll dough
2 tablespoons barbecue
   sauce
⅓ cup finely shredded
   sharp Cheddar cheese
8 hot dogs
¼ teaspoon poppy seeds
   (optional)
   Additional barbecue
   sauce (optional)

Gargoyle Tongues

½ teaspoon ground cumin
4 soft corn or flour tortillas
1 cup (4 ounces) finely
   shredded sharp
   Cheddar cheese
2 tablespoons chopped
   ripe olives
8 teaspoons salsa

1. Preheat oven to 450°F.

2. Sprinkle cumin evenly over tortillas; rub gently. Cut each tortilla into 4 wedges. Coat baking sheet with nonstick cooking spray. Arrange wedges on baking sheet, allowing space between wedges. Sprinkle cheese over wedges. (Allow cheese to spill over edges slightly.) Sprinkle with olives. Bake 4 minutes or until cheese is melted.

3. Remove from heat. Top each wedge with ½ teaspoon salsa.

Makes 16 wedges

Bourbon Street Beignet Puffs

Heat 2 or 3 inches CRISCO® Shortening to 365°F in deep fryer or deep saucepan. In a separate saucepan, combine water, butter and salt. Bring to a boil.

Add flour and sugar. Reduce heat to medium and stir until dough is smooth, glossy and comes away from side of pan. Remove from heat. Stir 2 minutes to cool slightly. Add eggs 1 at a time. Beat after each addition until well blended. Beat in vanilla.

Drop by teaspoonfuls, a few at a time, into hot CRISCO® Shortening. Fry several minutes or until deep golden brown. Turn as needed for even browning. Remove with slotted metal spoon. Drain on paper towels. Roll in confectioners' sugar. Serve warm.

Makes 2½ dozen

CRISCO® Shortening for deep frying
1 cup water
½ cup butter
¼ teaspoon salt
1 cup all-purpose flour
1 tablespoon plus 1½ teaspoons granulated sugar
4 eggs (at room temperature)
1½ teaspoons vanilla
Confectioners' sugar

Holiday Appetizer Puffs

1 sheet frozen puff pastry,
    thawed (½ of
    17¼-ounce package)
2 tablespoons olive or
    vegetable oil
Toppings: grated
    Parmesan cheese,
    sesame seeds, poppy
    seeds, dried dill weed,
    dried basil leaves,
    paprika, drained
    capers, pimiento-
    stuffed green olive
    slices

1. Preheat oven to 425°F. Roll out pastry on lightly floured surface to 13-inch square. Cut into shapes with cookie cutters. (Simple-shaped cutters work best.) Place on ungreased baking sheets.

2. Brush cut-outs lightly with oil. Decorate with desired toppings.

3. Bake 6 to 8 minutes or until golden. Serve warm or at room temperature.

Makes about 1½ dozen appetizers

Bubbling Cauldron

1. Melt cheese in medium saucepan over low heat, stirring occasionally. Remove from heat. Stir in beans, salsa and jalapeño peppers, if desired.

2. Carefully cut center out of bread, leaving 1½-inch-thick shell. Cut bread center into pieces for dipping.

3. Reserve 1 pretzel rod. Arrange remaining pretzel rods on serving plate to resemble campfire logs. Place bread cauldron on pretzels; fill with cheese dip, allowing some to spill over top of bread cauldron. Arrange bread pieces and cocktail bread around cauldron. Place reserved pretzel rod in cheese dip; serve immediately. *Makes 20 servings*

Tip: Use your favorite Halloween cookie cutters to cut scary shapes from the cocktail bread.

1 package (16 ounces) processed cheese
2 cans (15 ounces each) black beans, well drained
1 cup medium or hot salsa
1 can (4 ounces) diced jalapeño peppers, drained (optional)
2 loaves (18 ounces each) round marble rye bread, unsliced
   Pretzel rods
   Cocktail rye or pumpernickel bread slices

Pesto-Cheese Logs

1/3 cup walnuts, toasted*
1 package (8 ounces)
    cream cheese, softened
1/3 cup prepared pesto sauce
1/3 cup crumbled feta cheese
2 teaspoons cracked black
    pepper
2 tablespoons finely
    shredded carrot
2 tablespoons chopped
    fresh parsley
Assorted crackers
Carrot slivers, parsley
    and fresh thyme, for
    garnish (optional)

1. Process walnuts in food processor, using on/off pulsing action until walnuts are ground, but not pasty. Remove from food processor; set aside.

2. Process cream cheese, pesto and feta cheese in food processor until smooth. Remove 3/4 cup cheese mixture to waxed paper; form 4-inch log. Wrap waxed paper around cheese log. Repeat with remaining cheese mixture. Refrigerate logs at least 4 hours or until well chilled. Roll each chilled log to form 5-inch log.

3. Combine walnuts and pepper. Roll 1 log in nut mixture to coat. Combine 2 tablespoons carrot and 2 tablespoons parsley. Roll remaining log in carrot mixture to coat. Serve immediately, or wrap and refrigerate up to one day before serving. To serve, thinly slice log and serve with crackers. Garnish, if desired.

Makes 2 logs

To toast walnuts, spread in single layer on ungreased baking sheet. Bake in preheated 350°F oven 8 to 10 minutes or until golden brown, stirring frequently.

Barbecued Meatballs

Slow Cooker Directions

1. Preheat oven to 350°F. Combine ground beef, ⅓ cup ketchup, bread crumbs, egg, onion flakes, garlic salt and black pepper in medium bowl; mix lightly but thoroughly. Shape mixture into 1-inch meatballs. Place meatballs in 2 (15×10-inch) jelly-roll pans or shallow roasting pans. Bake 18 minutes or until browned. Transfer meatballs to slow cooker.

2. Mix remaining 1 cup ketchup, brown sugar, tomato paste, soy sauce, vinegar and hot pepper sauce in medium bowl. Pour over meatballs. Cover; cook on LOW 4 hours.

3. Serve with cocktail picks. Garnish with diced bell peppers, if desired.

Makes about 4 dozen meatballs

Barbecued Franks: Arrange 2 (12-ounce) packages or 3 (8-ounce) packages cocktail franks in slow cooker. Combine 1 cup ketchup with brown sugar, tomato paste, soy sauce, vinegar and hot pepper sauce in medium bowl; pour over franks. Cook according to directions for Barbecued Meatballs.

2 pounds 95% lean ground beef
1⅓ cups ketchup, divided
3 tablespoons seasoned dry bread crumbs
1 egg, lightly beaten
2 tablespoons dried onion flakes
¾ teaspoon garlic salt
½ teaspoon black pepper
1 cup packed light brown sugar
1 can (6 ounces) tomato paste
¼ cup soy sauce
¼ cup cider vinegar
1½ teaspoons hot pepper sauce
Diced bell peppers (optional)

8 hard-cooked eggs
8 small tomato slices
8 wooden toothpicks
   Mayonnaise
8 small pimiento-stuffed
   green olives
8 black peppercorns
   Parsley
16 whole cloves

Yolkensteins

1. Cut thin slice from wide end of egg, allowing egg to stand upright. Then slice egg horizontally, about ⅓ up from bottom.

2. Place tomato slice on bottom piece of egg. Insert toothpick upright in middle of tomato slice and egg for "spine." Reattach top piece of egg.

3. Using dabs of mayonnaise, attach slices of olives for "eyes" and peppercorn for "nose." Attach parsley for "hair." Insert 1 whole clove on each side of egg under tomato slice for "bolts." Pipe mayonnaise "teeth" onto tomato slice just before serving. Repeat for all eggs. *Makes 8 servings*

Festive Holidays

Cheesy Christmas Trees

1. Preheat broiler. Combine mayonnaise and salad dressing mix in medium bowl. Add cheeses; mix well.

2. Using large cookie cutters, cut bread slices into Christmas tree shapes. Spread each tree with about 1 tablespoon mayonnaise mixture. Decorate with red and green bell pepper strips. Place on baking sheet.

3. Broil 4 inches from heat 2 to 3 minutes or until bubbling. Serve warm.

Makes about 12 appetizers

½ cup mayonnaise

1 tablespoon dry ranch-style salad dressing mix

1 cup shredded Cheddar cheese

¼ cup grated Parmesan cheese

12 slices firm white bread

¼ cup red bell pepper strips

¼ cup green bell pepper strips

Celebration Cheese Ball

2 packages (8 ounces each) cream cheese, softened
⅓ cup mayonnaise
¼ cup grated Parmesan cheese
2 tablespoons finely chopped carrot
1 tablespoon finely chopped red onion
1½ teaspoons prepared horseradish
¼ teaspoon salt
½ cup chopped pecans or walnuts
Assorted crackers and breadsticks

1. Combine all ingredients except pecans and crackers in medium bowl. Cover; refrigerate until firm.

2. Shape cheese mixture into ball; roll in pecans. Wrap cheese ball in plastic wrap; refrigerate at least 1 hour.

3. Serve with assorted crackers and breadsticks.

Makes about 2½ cups

Tasty Tombstones

1. Pierce potatoes in several places with fork. Microwave at HIGH, 2 minutes per potato. (Total time may vary according to microwave capacity.) Let cool 5 minutes. Slice each potato in half lengthwise.

2. Heat olive oil in large skillet over medium heat. Add potato halves; cook until tender and slightly browned. Remove from heat. Cut each potato in half lengthwise again to form 2 smaller tombstones.

3. Form rows of bacon, onion, cheese and olives in 13×9-inch pan or decorative dish to resemble paths through a graveyard. Place several potato tombstones upright randomly throughout dish. (Decorate, if desired.) Spoon ketchup or salsa at base of each potato. Using pastry bag or resealable plastic food storage bag with corner removed, pipe sour cream in ghost shapes throughout dish. Sprinkle chopped parsley throughout dish to represent grass, if desired. Serve remaining potatoes in separate dish. *Makes 6 servings*

6 large baking potatoes
¼ cup olive oil
1½ tablespoons paprika
8 slices bacon, crisp-cooked and crumbled
1 cup chopped green onions
2 cups shredded Cheddar cheese
1 cup chopped black olives
1 cup ketchup or salsa
1 cup sour cream
Chopped parsley (optional)

Eggy Eyeballs

12 hard-cooked eggs, peeled and halved lengthwise
1 package (8 ounces) cream cheese
½ cup finely chopped yellow onion
½ cup finely chopped ham or turkey
¼ cup milk
⅛ teaspoon salt
⅛ teaspoon garlic powder
24 small pimiento-stuffed green olives
Shredded red cabbage
12 baby carrots

1. Remove egg yolks from egg halves; reserve yolks for another use. Combine cream cheese, onion, ham, milk, salt and garlic powder in small bowl; mix well.

2. Fill each egg center with about 1 tablespoon cream cheese mixture. Place olive (pimiento straight up) in center of each egg; press slightly.

3. Place cabbage on serving platter; arrange egg halves on top in pairs to resemble "eyes." Place 1 carrot below center of each pair to resemble "nose."

Makes 24 servings

Sheriff's Best Shot Sandwiches

1. Mound cream cheese in center of large serving platter; cover with red peppers. Reserve 2 baby pickles. Insert remaining pickles into cream cheese to resemble "cactus."

2. Top 4 bread slices with ham, 4 with turkey and 4 with cheese. Use 2-inch cookie cutter in shape of heart or sheriff's badge to cut shapes out of each sandwich bottom. Cut remaining 12 slices bread into same shapes for sandwich tops. Arrange around platter. Slice 2 reserved pickles crosswise into thin circles; place 1 slice in center of each sandwich.

3. To serve, allow guests to top each sandwich bottom with cream cheese spread and roasted red peppers and cover with cut-out bread tops.

Makes 12 servings

1 container (8 ounces) chive and onion cream cheese spread
¹⁄₃ cup chopped roasted red peppers
14 (1-inch-long) baby dill pickles
24 slices (2 inches square) cocktail rye or pumpernickel bread
4 slices deli ham
4 slices deli turkey
4 slices American, Muenster or Swiss cheese

Jack-O'-Lantern Cheese Ball

2 cups (8 ounces) shredded Cheddar cheese
½ (8-ounce) package cream cheese, softened
¼ cup solid-pack pumpkin
¼ cup pineapple preserves
¼ teaspoon ground allspice
¼ teaspoon ground nutmeg
1 pretzel rod, broken in half
　 Dark rye bread, red bell pepper, black olive slices and fresh parsley
　 Assorted crackers

1. Beat cheese, cream cheese, pumpkin, preserves and spices in medium bowl until smooth. Cover; refrigerate 2 to 3 hours or until cheese is firm enough to shape.

2. Shape mixture into round pumpkin; place on serving plate. Using knife, score vertical lines down pumpkin. Place pretzel rod in top for stem.

3. Cut bread into triangles for eyes. Decorate pumpkin, using bread, pepper slices, olives and parsley. Cover loosely; refrigerate until serving time. Serve with crackers. *Makes 16 to 18 servings*

Festive Holidays

Spicy Sweet & Sour Cocktail Franks

Slow Cooker Directions

1. Combine all ingredients in slow cooker; mix well.

2. Cover; cook on LOW 2 to 3 hours.

3. Serve warm or at room temperature with cocktail picks and additional hot pepper sauce, if desired. *Makes about 4 dozen cocktail franks*

2 packages (8 ounces each) cocktail franks
½ cup ketchup or chili sauce
½ cup apricot preserves
1 teaspoon hot pepper sauce
Additional hot pepper sauce (optional)

Rosemary Pork with Vampire Fighter's Garlic

Pork

2 pork tenderloins (about 1 pound each)

Juice of 2 lemons

1 tablespoon extra-virgin olive oil

½ teaspoon dried rosemary leaves

Paprika

Salt

Black pepper

Aioli

½ cup mayonnaise

2 tablespoons olive oil

2 tablespoons Dijon mustard

1 clove garlic, minced

⅛ teaspoon salt

1. Preheat oven to 425°F. Place tenderloins in 13×9-inch baking pan; pour lemon juice over top. Drizzle pork with oil; sprinkle with rosemary, paprika, salt and pepper. Let stand 15 minutes to marinate.

2. Meanwhile, combine aioli ingredients in small mixing bowl; cover with plastic wrap. Refrigerate until ready to serve.

3. Tuck under thin end of pork. Bake 25 minutes or until barely pink in center and meat thermometer inserted into thickest part registers 160°F. *Do not overcook.* Remove from oven and let stand 5 minutes. Transfer pork to cutting board; thinly slice. Arrange on serving platter. Drizzle pan juices over slices. Serve warm with aioli. *Makes 24 servings*

Pecan Cheese Ball

1. Combine cream cheese, parsley, chives, Worcestershire sauce and hot pepper sauce in medium bowl. Cover; refrigerate until firm.

2. Form cheese mixture into 12 (1½-inch) balls. Roll each ball in chopped herbs, paprika or pecans. Store tightly wrapped in plastic wrap in refrigerator.

3. Allow cheese balls to soften at room temperature before serving with crackers. *Makes 12 cheese balls*

Variation: Form cheese mixture into one large ball. Roll in pecans.

1 package (8 ounces)
   cream cheese, softened
¼ cup finely chopped fresh
   parsley
2 tablespoons finely
   chopped fresh chives
½ teaspoon Worcestershire
   sauce
   Dash hot pepper sauce
   Finely chopped fresh
   herbs (parsley,
   watercress or basil)
   Paprika
   Finely chopped pecans
   Assorted crackers

Abracadabra Hats

1 package crescent dinner
rolls (8 rolls)
½ teaspoon dried basil
leaves (optional)
16 turkey pepperoni slices
3 to 4 salami sticks, cut
into 2-inch pieces
2 cups pizza or marinara
sauce

1. Preheat oven to 375°F. Separate dough; place individual pieces on work surface. Gently shape each piece into tall triangle. Sprinkle basil evenly over all, if desired.

2. Using biscuit cutter or knife, cut each pepperoni slice into 2 crescents. Place 1 salami stick piece along base of each dough triangle. Roll up dough to completely cover salami, about one third of way up, to make hat "brim."

3. Arrange 2 pepperoni crescents on top part of each "hat." Place "hats" on nonstick cookie sheet. Bake 12 minutes or until edges are slightly golden. Meanwhile, warm sauce in small saucepan. Serve "hats" with sauce for dipping.

Makes 8 servings

Acknowledgments

*The publisher would like to thank the companies and organizations listed below
for the use of their recipes and photographs in this publication.*

ACH FOOD COMPANIES, INC.

Birds Eye® Foods

Chef Paul Prudhomme's Magic Seasoning Blends®

Crisco is a registered trademark of The J.M. Smucker Company

Del Monte Corporation

Guiltless Gourmet®

The Hidden Valley® Food Products Company

Hillshire Farm®

Hormel Foods, LLC

Lawry's® Foods

McIlhenny Company (TABASCO® brand Pepper Sauce)

National Chicken Council / US Poultry & Egg Association

National Pork Board

Ortega®, A Division of B&G Foods, Inc.

Reckitt Benckiser Inc.

StarKist Seafood Company

Unilever Foods North America

Index

Index